Poetry Ireland Review 76

Eagarthóir / Editor **Eva Bourke**

© Copyright Poetry Ireland Ltd. 2003

Poetry Ireland Ltd./Éigse Éireann Teo. gratefully acknowledges the assistance of The Arts Council/An Chomhairle Ealaíon, the Arts Council of Northern Ireland, and FÁS.

Patrons of Poetry Ireland/Éigse Éireann

Grogan's Castle Lounge
Eastern Washington University
Dillon Murphy & Co.
Office Of Public Works
Richard Murphy
Occidental Tourist Ltd.
Winding Stair Bookshop
Doirín Meagher
The Irish-American Poetry Society

Desmond Windle
Joan & Joe McBreen
Fearon, O'Neill, Rooney
Daig Quinn
Twomey Steo Ltd.
Kevin Connolly
Neville Keery
Swan Training Institute

Poetry Ireland invites individuals, cultural groups and commercial organisations to become Patrons. Patrons are entitled to reclaim tax at their highest rate for all donations of between €128.00 and €12,700. For more details please contact the Director, at Bermingham Tower, Dublin Castle, Dublin 2, Ireland or phone 01 6714632 or e-mail: **management@poetryireland.ie**

Poetry Ireland Review is published quarterly by Poetry Ireland Ltd. The Editor enjoys complete autonomy in the choice of material published. The contents of this publication should not be taken to reflect either the views or the policy of the publishers.

ISSN: 0332-2998
ISBN: 1-902121-14-7

Assistant Editors: Paul Lenehan and Kendra Eash (Boston University)
Cover Template: Colm Ó Cannain
Typography: Barry Hannigan
Cover Photo: The photo depicts a battle scene from the Trojan War, from an image supplied by Eva Bourke

Printed in Ireland by **ColourBooks Ltd.**, Baldoyle Industrial Estate, Dublin 13.

Contents
Poetry Ireland Review 76

	4	**Editorial**
Mary O'Donoghue	6	Good Speech
John F Deane	7	The Instruments of Art
Melanie Challenger	12	Garden Tomb
Lucy Brennan	13	Cold Skies
Jesse Lee Kercheval	14	Magdalena at The Prado
Giles Goodland	16	A Glimmer
Knute Skinner	18	Slow Motions
Michael Brophy	19	Walking the Dog
Jo Pestel	20	The Blue Ball
	21	Foursquare
Denise Blake	22	Breathe
Paul Maddern	23	Effacé
	23	The Ulster Way
	23	Kinetics
Patrick Cotter	24	Californian Girl
Lynda Horgan	25	Piazza
	25	The Kiss
Howard Wright	26	A Brief Look at the Weather
Fred Johnston	27	Mills
Gerard Murphy	28	The Last Days in the History of Love
David Meagher	30	Brazilians
Carolyn Jess	31	Postcards
Tommy Curran	32	Venus at Home
Aimée Sands	33	The League of the One-Breasted Women
Gary Allen	34	Bethlehem down
Moya Cannon	35	Walking out to Islandeddy
Joan McBreen	36	Knockma in Spring
Nessa O'Mahony	37	To my dear biographer
Art Murphy	38	Lachrymae Rerum
	39	Elsewhere
William Oxley	40	No Real Present
	41	The South Country
George Evans	42	Girls in the Trees
Eamon Grennan	43	Mid-May's Eldest Child
Gerard Beirne	44	Properties of Solutions: The Colloidal State
Eugenio Montale	46	The Mirages
Ann Killough	48	The Birdfeeder

Ivy Bannister	50	Appetite
Alice Lyons	51	The Polish Language
Rody Gorman	52	Dosan den Fheamainn Bhuí
	52	Ealta Fearbóg
Annie Deppe	53	Night Voices
Daisy Zamora	54	Proposal
Bei Dao	55	Black Map

Poets on War

Aileen Kelly	57	Documentary
Fred Johnston	58	War Poem for the Anxious
Susan Wicks	59	Christmas
Danny Hardisty	60	The Airman
Patrick Cotter	62	Letter to Charles Simic, April 1999
Fergus Allen	64	On Wexford Bridge
Kieran Furey	71	How Rome Rises as it Ruins
Michael Brophy	72	View from the Gun
Leland Bardwell	73	The Invisible from Iraq to the USA
Fred Marchant	74	ars poetica
	75	Collateral
	75	The Shelter
T Michael Sullivan	76	First Snow
Kevin Bowen	77	The Post-Nuclear Age
John F Deane	78	The Aftertaste of Bitterness
Rita Ann Higgins	81	Grandchildren
Ger Killeen	82	Sometimes Instead of a Poem
Mary Branley	84	Wait for me
Ciaran O'Driscoll	86	A Gift for the President
Medbh McGuckian	88	Picasso's Windows
Michael Coady	90	Twelve Warm Coats, 1802
Vincent Woods	91	On being asked to write a poem against the war
	91	Bitter Legend
Denis Collins	92	The Peace
Doug Anderson	94	Phan Thiet
	95	The Torturer's Apprentice
Jo Slade	96	Pegasus Bridge, Benoville, France: 09/07/99
Huu Thinh	97	Asking
George Evans	98	Addendum Constitution Erratum
Ann Killough	98	Anniversary (September 11, 2002)
Daisy Zamora	100	When I See Them Passing By

Deirdre Brennan	101	Ar iarraidh
Bei Dao	102	Ramallah
Anna Woodford	103	Guernica
John E Smelcer	104	This Is Just To Say

German Poetry in Translation

Paul Celan	106	Anabasis
	107	Glimmer-Tree
Ilse Aichinger	108	City Centre
	108	Jews' Lane
Brigitte Oleschinski	109	Seaweed Frozen
Johannes Bobrowski	110	Memorial Leaf
	111	Elderflower
Ingeborg Bachmann	112	No Delicacies
	114	Bohemia Lies On The Sea
Erich Fried	115	Questions About Poetry After Auschwitz
	116	Journalists' Club
Hans Magnus Enzensberger	117	The Great Goddess
	118	Equisetum
	119	The Declaration of War Explained
W.G. Sebald	120	*from* Elementargedicht Nach der Natur
Silke Scheuermann	123	Requiem for a Recently-Conquered Planet with Intensive Radiation
Sarah Kirsch	124	Vanishing Point
	125	The Plain
Michael Krüger	126	Night Flight
	127	At First Glance
Durs Grünbein	128	Monologic Poem No. 2
	129	September Elegies
Peter Waterhouse	130	Into The Great Entanglement Outside Vienna
Thomas Böhme	132	So Many
Sabine Küchler	124	So Much

David Butler	135	**Precision and Restraint**
Ciaran O'Driscoll	140	**Memorable Truth-Telling**
Clíodhna Carney	145	**Poets and Makers**
Adrian Frazier	150	**Life in Leitrim**

Notes on Contributors 152

Editorial/Eagarfhocal

This 76th *Poetry Ireland Review* will be the last issue in the familiar unmistakable design, with its matte covers featuring an atmospheric photograph in tastefully subdued colour. It will soon return somewhat altered in format and looks, but as fresh and full of vitality as ever, of that I have no doubt.

Since its beginnings in Autumn, 1962 (as *Poetry Ireland*, edited by John Jordan), *PIR* has become an internationally acclaimed publication, and has honoured this in characteristic non-insular fashion by devoting entire issues or sections of issues to the poetry of other languages in translation – Argentinian for instance, or Palestinian, and, in this issue, German poetry. Openness towards other cultures denotes a healthy confidence devoid of self-congratulatory provincialism, and it was with this thought in my mind that I went to work on the selection and translation of 25 poems by 15 poets from Austria and Germany, knowing that it would be impossible to give more than a taste of what occurred in German language poetry since the collapse of the Thousand Year Reich.

The freedom to choose what I personally loved was wonderful, but needless to say the poems chosen reflect only a tiny fraction of the debate going on during the almost miraculous period of recovery in German intellectual life from the sixties and seventies up to the present. They can only give an inkling of the frequently harsh controversies about the role of poetry in a world which must be interpreted in political and economic terms. This epoch of political radicalism was followed by a quieter, more introspective time of inwardness and subjectivity, and with a new generation of poets emerging, who made their literary débuts in the nineties, German poetry has entered upon a renewed phase of experimentalism, which has rediscovered and appropriated the avant-garde traditions of Dada, and of the iconoclasts of Vienna.

It has become urban, streetwise, ironic, defying expectations of what poetry should be, become pluralistic and multi-cultural, taking its cue from popular and drug culture. Language experimentation – collage, quote, slang and splintered syntax – has moved into the foreground again. The role of Berlin as centre of ultra-cool and grungy chic, towards which the new poets gravitate, is important, and the prevailing tone of the new avant-garde is anti-classical, anti-linear, and anti-discursive. These few examples of the work of younger poets can, however, not attempt to give much of an idea of this, simply because such experimentalism frequently also defies translation – perhaps Durs Grünbein's 'Monologic Poem 2' or Brigitte Oleschinski's poem may serve as an example here. However, I also discovered during my research a welcome return to playfulness and humour, as Waterhouse, Böhme and Küchler demonstrate.

I want to take this opportunity to thank my friend, the experienced translator and poet Peter Jankowski, who is equally at home in the literature of Germany as in that of Ireland, for his invaluable help, his clear-eyed and perceptive reading of both originals and translations, and his many excellent suggestions towards the improvement of a translation.

This *PIR* is divided into three sections: a general selection from the submissions of the past few months, poems on war – interestingly enough many submissions sent to PIR naturally fell under the category of war poem – and the German poets. I want to express my gratitude to everyone who responded so generously to my invitation to contribute a poem on the subject of war. My feeling that many would welcome the opportunity to express their concern and opposition was proved correct.

I also would like to thank the staff of Poetry Ireland, who are to vacate their airy premises in Dublin Castle and are faced with homelessness, for their invariably friendly and consistent support. May the Arts Council and the City of Dublin demonstrate their appreciation of their hard work and idealism by re-housing them swiftly and in the most satisfactory way.

Eva Bourke

Mary O'Donoghue

Good Speech

What is Good Speech?
Good Speech
is Speaking Out
Clearly and Distinctly
with Proper Emphasis
and Expression.

Ay!   Eee!   Eye!   Oh!   You!
First verse of "Norman the Zebra
at the Zoo." We are fourteen
and we hate Wednesdays,

for we must lose
our muckle-mouthedness
and become Violet Elizabeth Botts,
sugaring and plumming our epiglottis.

*Th*is, *Th*at, *Th*ese and *Th*ose *Th*istles.
Lose the lisps, and the gap-toothed
whistles. Soft and hard palate?
Search around in some
boy's mouth to find them.

"The Marrog from Mars" lurches
his way through the nightmares
of the girl in our class
with a stammer.

We are dulcet.
We are pregnant
in our pauses,
as silver-tongued
as Demosthenes
or Audrey Hepburn.

We secrete honey.
We pantomime.
We make eye contact.
We make ourselves sick.

John F Deane

The Instruments of Art

We move in draughty, barn-like spaces, swallows
busy round the beams, like images. There is room
for larger canvases to be displayed, there are storing-places
for our weaker efforts; hold

to warm clothing, to surreptitious nips of spirits
hidden behind the instruments of art. It is all, ultimately,
a series of bleak self-portraits, of measured-out
reasons for living. Sketches

of heaven and hell. Self-portrait with computer;
self-portrait, nude, with blanching flesh; self
as Lazarus, mid-summons, as Job, mid-scream.
There is outward

dignity, white shirt, black tie, a black hat
held before the crotch; within, the turmoil, and advanced
decay. Each work achieved and signed announcing itself
the last. The barn door slammed shut.

*

There was a pungency of remedies on the air, the house
hushed for weeks, attending. A constant focus
on the sick-room. When I went in, fingers reached for me,
like cray-fish bones; saliva

hung in the cave of the mouth like a web. Later,
with sheets and eiderdown spirited away, flowers stood
fragrant in a vase in the purged room. Still life. Leaving
a recurring sensation of dread, a greyness

like a dye, darkening the page; that *Dies Irae*, a slow
fret-saw wailing of black-vested priests. It was Ireland
subservient, relishing its purgatory. Books, indexed,
locked in glass cases. Night

I could hear the muted rhythms in the dance-hall; bicycles
slack against a gable-wall; bicycle-clips, minerals, the raffle;
words hesitant, ill-used, like groping. In me the dark bloom
of fascination, an instilled withdrawal.

*

He had a long earth-rake and he drew lines
like copy-book pages on which he could write
seeds, meaning – love; and can you love, be loved, and never
say 'love', never hear 'love'?

The uncollected apples underneath the trees
moved with legged things and a chocolate-coloured rust;
if you speak out flesh and heart's desire will the naming of it
canker it? She cut hydrangeas,

placed them in a pewter bowl (allowing herself at times
to cry) close by the tabernacle door; patience in pain
mirroring creation's order. The boy, suffering puberty, sensed
in his flesh a small revulsion, and held

*

hands against his crotch in fear. Paint the skin
a secret-linen white with a smart stubble of dirt. The first
fountain-pen, the paint-box, pristine tablets of Prussian Blue,
of Burnt Sienna – words

sounding in the soul like organ-music, Celeste and Diapason –
and that brush-tip, its animated bristles; he began at once
painting the dark night of grief, as if the squirrel's tail
could empty the ocean onto sand. Life-

drawing, with naked girl, half-light of inherited faith,
colour it in, and rhyme it, blue. In the long library, stooped
over the desks, we read cosmology, the reasoning
of Aquinas; we would hold

the knowledge of the whole world within us. The dawn
chorus: *laudetur Jesus Christus*: and the smothered,
smothering answer: *in aeternum. Amen.* Loneliness
hanging about our frames, like cassocks.

*

The words of God grew angry about my head, like wasps; it is hard
to shake off darkness, the black habit. New world; sky at sunset –
fire-red, opening its mouth to scream; exploration of the belly-flesh
of a lover. It was like

the rubbling of revered buildings, the moulding of words
into new shapes. In the cramped cab of a truck she, first time,
fleshed across his knees; the kiss, two separate, not singular,
alive. It was death already, prowling

at the dark edge of the wood, fangs bared, saliva-white.
Sometimes you fear insanity, the bridge humming to your scream
(oil, casein, pastel) but there is nobody to hear, the streaming river
only, and the streaming sky; soon

on a dark night, the woman tearing dumbly at her hair while you
gaze uselessly onto ashes. Helpless again you fear
woman: saint and whore and hapless devotee. Paint your words
deep violet, pale yellow,

*

the fear, *Winter in Meath, Fugue, the Apotheosis of Desire.*
The terror is not to be able to write. Naked and virginal
she embraced the skeleton and was gone. What, now,
is the colour of *God is love*

when they draw the artificial grass over the hole, the rains
hold steady, and the diggers wait impatiently under trees? Too long
disturbing presences were shadowing the page, the bleak
ego-walls, like old galvanize

round the festering; that artificial mess collapsing
down on her, releasing a small, essential spirit, secular
bone-structure, the fingers reaching out of *need*, no longer *will*.
Visceral edge of ocean,

wading things, the agitated ooze, women on the jetty
watching out to sea; at last, I, too, could look
out into the world again; the woman, dressed in blue, who
broke from the group on the jetty and came

*

purposefully towards us, I watched through stained glass of the door,
and loved her. Mine the religion of poetry, the poetry
of religion, the worthy Academicians unwilling to realize
we don't live off neglect. Is there

a way to understand the chaos of the human heart? our
slaughters, our carelessness, our unimaginable wars?
Without a God can we win some grace? Will our canvases,
their patterns, and forms, their

rhymes and rhythms, supply a modicum of worth?
The old man dragged himself up the altar steps,
beginning the old rites; the thurible clashed against its chain;
we rose, dutifully, though they

have let us down again, holding their forts
against new hordes; I had hoped the canvas would be filled
with radiant colours, but the word God became a word
of scorn, easiest to ignore. We

*

came out again, our heartache unassuaged.
The high corral of the Academy, too, is loud with gossipers,
the ego-traffickers, nothing to be expected there. Self-
portrait, with grief

and darkening sky. Soon it will be the winter studio; a small
room, enclosed; you will sit, stilled, on a wooden chair, tweed
heavy about your frame, eyes focused inwards, where there is
no past, no future; you sit alone,

your papers in an ordered disarray; images stilled, like nests,
emptied; the phone beside you will not ring; nor will the light
come on; everything depends on where your eyes
focus; when

the darkness comes, drawing its black
drape across the window, there will remain
the stillness of paint, words on the page, the laid down
instruments of your art.

Melanie Challenger

Garden Tomb

I am trying to find you,
but the book has no map. I hear you singing,
Loosen little slums of soil, snick the sacks of clay.

I am here. Listen.

A road-building force is tearing up
the ground and I root amongst the litter,
find only the clack of bone-boxes,
slambang limestone.

I know you are there,
murmuring through tussocks, singing
through tablets. Hide-and-seek is an old game.

Sometimes when I am about to give up,
I fancy I catch sight of you.
Listen. My voice is a grass-whistle.

I am here. Listen.

Lucy Brennan

Cold Skies

It was not in her nature
to rage as he did. She dreaded
her small explosions: word-shrapnel.
But when the clouds darkened
over her children
their last unsteady bridge collapsed.

He discovered eventually
that he had left no pathway
to return by. It was a new feeling;
to be islanded. Happy,
at first, with the adventure,
his star-filled sky soon turned cold.

She felt the approach of winter
in the silent frost of mornings.
Snow's indifference at evening
erased all lines of communication
and blanketed a battle-field
where both lay powerless.

War was officially declared
long after the exchange of hostilities.
The terms of surrender
were to their mutual disadvantage.
Costs were paid in full
and irrecoverable by all concerned.

Jesse Lee Kercheval

Magdalena at The Prado

We are rushing, our children in tow,
to see what we're supposed to see,
Goya's *Saturn Devouring One of His Children*,
Bosch's *Garden of Earthly Delights*. But
Magdalena, ten, whose Nikes never stop –
stops, transfixed before a triptych
of Jesus' life. 15th Century Dutch,
my eye tells me, not the highlight
of this collection, but a clear rendition
of a familiar subject. But not to Magdalena,
raised by a Unitarian and a lapsed
Episcopalian. In Wisconsin,
she asked me if the Buddha at our local
Chinese restaurant was Christ.

Now, her father takes time to explain
the Immaculate Conception, how the word of God,
a ribbon of ecstasy, winds from the Angel's
trumpet into Mary's gentle, upturned ear.
Magdalena nods, approving – finds this
more believable than the penises and vaginas
she's been taught since kindergarten.
God signs his name, a son is born. Like
cashing a check at the drive-thru window,
word turned to golden flesh.

But she is drawn more to death,
neglecting the baby Jesus in his high
Gothic manger for the tiny, dashed bodies
of the Massacre of the Innocents.
For Jesus on the cross, all muscled agony,
the bleeding thieves beside him.

And Jesus risen, poking a single, curious
finger into his gaping side, as if searching
for a coin lost in his pocket. In the triptych,
he steps out of his cold tomb
like Magdalena escaping onto the playground
after a long, grey day at school.
She heads home to her parents, baby brother.
Jesus ascends to his father, knowing
his mother will come home later. To her,
it makes all kinds of perfect sense.

Then she's on the move again,
rubber soles squeaking against marble.
If I cannot hold her, my Magdalena,
how, possibly, could Hell? She flits
past the gilded portraits of the saints
and their glorious demises. Stephen
being stoned, Catherine broken on
her wheel. What is death but a night
when you sleep long and well and wake,
taller, stronger, ready for fifth grade
or the next life, which ever gets here faster.

Stop a sec, sweetie, her father says, in this gallery
of portraits, *let me take your picture.*
Magdalena throws wide her arms
among the gold and painted glory,
St Andrew dying on his cross behind her,
the X that marks the spot.

Giles Goodland

A Glimmer

The windscreen wiper keeps rewriting
the future until the mist blows free, leaving
a distant edginess on the road, a haze.
Each car tows an after-image of rain.

For the last 40 miles she's been making
zooming noises, some of them words.
Then she asks *Does everything in the world
have a name?* I think of instancing

the way light shines through pines
just after the morning's tissue-wrap
has lifted. The car's rhythm of
cerebral grey noise. The mixed sense

of loss and fragility, doing 80
in a small car on the long run
back to her home. The expressions
that ghost over the morning, from bored

to dreamy. The borders of language
against which we bounce, which thicken
around unspoken stories in this
ceremony of naming that lasts

as long as childhood and which
she's beginning to see is only limited
by what exists. As when a spaceship
achieves hyperdrive (not every name

in the world has a thing) this curvy
substance unsticks, as if the motorway
could dissolve into the words it is made of.
Fields bend beside the traffic's windrows.

I wheedle some decent music out of
the car radio. This is an answer,
but not the right one. There are riches
inside our empty pockets, weighing down

our open palms, effervescing in the mouth,
bursting before this utterness. Even
to answer her requires moving from
the fast lane in which we are stuck.

Knute Skinner

Slow Motions

As the car slowed down,
turning into my driveway,
he let go of my hand
and shifted gears.
A light rain had begun to fall,
and we sat in the car kissing
as it beaded the windshield.
Then came the downpour.

In the kitchen we sat side by side
drinking hot chocolate.
His shirt and trousers were drying,
draped over a tubular chair
by the wood stove;
my dress, from a hook on the door,
dripped on the tiles.
We spoke just a few words,
about trifling matters.

Later, the rain turned to hail.
We turned our faces upward
in the absolute dark
as if we could see the hailstones
as they beat on the skylight.
Then he resumed his slow motions,
easing, easing away
and then gently pressing.

The wind that followed found out
each crevice in the old cottage,
now whistling a tune, now moaning.
He breathed deep as he sprawled
half over my body.
When I rolled him onto his side,
he stirred and muttered.
I spooned my body to his
and kissed his shoulder.

Michael Brophy

Walking the Dog

Our first dog
Was a Corgi
That hunted for hedgehogs
In a garden in England.

Then there was the stray
In Seychelles which
Barked at dead bats
On telegraph wires.

Next there was the Abso
In Africa,
Dodging across the desert
As he was dive-bombed
By vultures.

Tonight, it's an Arab sheep dog
Snarling at scorpions.

Taking out the dog
Instead of my temper,
Our arguments, my love,
Could span the world.

Jo Pestel

The Blue Ball

Because you loved the idea of me
before I came and had a template ready,
and because I arrived spiky
and spilling over, somehow the big ball
we threw between us bright
and bouncing on the hard-ribbed sand
at Tramore, me shrieking, you
younger than other fathers
as you pounded after me
the insides of your arms smooth
and sticky when you jumped way higher
and the smell of you, hot and big –
somehow that ball got lost
bobbing away on some tide or maybe
caught in bladderwrack on a back strand
or stuck fast out of sight between rocks;
and when we got home and shook out
the sand and unpacked our lives,
there it wasn't

Jo Pestel

Foursquare

When the moon squints through the skylight
my four angels bristle, sigh, change places. They know
I lie for hours beneath my sloping ceiling, head blazing
with scraps, colours, harmonies, the wisps of things

and that come Samhain I'll stay quiet all winter
and listen to dead breaths from leaves, dream of Archangel,
the music of snow, icicles radiant through pines;
that though Matthew, Mark, Luke and John hummed in my ear

I chased dragons, unicorns, phoenix, tortoise; they know
that I admire the Lightbearer and long to be magnificent in failure
but never had the guts to grab a whirlwind; that I hesitated
in night watches, at crossroads, headed off in all directions;

and speaking of guts, who will select my entrails
and place the four Canopic jars of all that's left of me?
Will they know I came from warmed stones,
that each spring I waited for the feast of quickening?

Denise Blake

Breathe

Mum used to say to us, *take a deep breath*
when we reached the point of our Sunday drive:
Lough Salt; Magheraroarty; Ards' Forest Park.

A returned emigrant who needed to breathe in
the whole of our county, purify her city-clogged
soul. Home colour returning to her cheeks.

I took a breath yesterday when that letter arrived
for Miss McGlinchey. The "Miss" dragging me back,
way before my childhood. Mum's communion half-crown

has now reached final savings. There has been interest
labouring all this time, labouring thirty years past
her time: "and we do not appear to have received a reply."

I Sunday-drove to Dunlewy today. A sorrow-cold
air held all of the valley in one eternal state.
Clouded heavens reflected in the lake's Madonna blue
as the pulsing wind whispered, *take a deep breath.*

Paul Maddern

Effacé
– for Nora

You had a face I could have lived a lie for;
That might have brought about the 2 point 4,
Not your sterile A4 annual report
About the daughter's aptitude for sport,
Ted's reunion and the dress you wore.
I want to know: did the dress allow
For seductive *développés* and *port de bras*,
Did sling-backs reveal triumphant arches,
Did you leave accountants conscious
And the husband damning Terpsichore?
But would I be content if my Odette
Was happy to distract suburban courts?
Nibble canapés, my swan. Forget
A mincing prince who remembers more.

The Ulster Way

Today their road did rise before them
But they missed the meaning in the old cliché.
Then their mothers led them through it
Step by step, explaining bricks and stones.
And class commenced before the bell.

Kinetics

The concrete's failed; its brutality abstracted
When I scream, "Ich bin ein Belfaster!"
For once it's seen the comic side it softens
And all around the stones begin to falter.

Patrick Cotter

Californian Girl
– for Beverly Parayno

You are the why of appetite.
More-of-you is beyond beautiful.
Love drips here and I drink.
Your mouth, the purse of my tongue,
your limbs lie quiet and musky on my drying skin.
No thoughts do I give now to your relentless warriors.
When alone, I hear their footfalls stamping towards infamy:
a hard chorus of hob-nailed leather
rapping over the planet's byways.
Earlier I swam through my own sweat to breach you,
to source your core, stripping away,
ripple by ripple, the lappings of pleasure.

If I seed you, will our child
roll in fear at the sound of your brothers' flight?
Whatever answer, I will love you,
even as the bayonet carves at my throat,
even as our son swathes himself in stars
and the colours of the barbershop,
sing allegiance to the dollar,
to the constitution of the bullet and the gun.

Lynda Horgan

Piazza

I tread the back alleys of your mind
praying for one moment
where I could sit
and take a second unshared with you
the words would be simple
I'd brush my lips
over them gently
and leave you there
with the next breeze
to tread the back alleys
for another thousand years

The Kiss

Anger
has a wall with tousled hair
and red red lipstick
seeps
to those cracks
on which I dwindle

like the last droplet
on an early morning cobweb

sucked in by the gentle movement
of a single, white tooth
surface now
slightly damp, slightly
pale
slightly

to stain those lips again
would be to kill

Howard Wright

A Brief Look at the Weather

God has a finger in every pie. His fist descends
on Carnmoney and Cavehill. He wipes the eye
of Carrickfergus, and diggers and haulers straighten
at rockpools, mesmerised by the change in the day.
A cold quickening. An edge-of-the-world gathering.
Air off the lough like a final breath. The skirts
of showers lift for the hills and erase them.
Now curlews worry the receding tide and oystercatchers
struggle to keep their heads as, under pressure,
families move further up the beach and bring a football
into play, the fathers making it arch and loop
as if calling down the tons of rain they are already
running from. It's the beginning of the end.
The cars slip like rats between the houses at teatime.

Fred Johnston

Mills

Give him his mills and their consequences
Of derelict rooms a football-pitch in length,
Strutted ceilings flush against a curve of stars:
These are his miracles of red brick and iron
Paned glass in squares banged out by local boys
And the great black gates hanging on their rust
The chimney like a finger scratching God's eye
Up in the Presbyterian vigours of the Bann
In their silence much more frightening now
Than when outside toilets and a whitewashed
Wall was being prosperous; they still have grace
Heavy as an oath, squatting in the ploughed pews,
Still full of themselves, like hymnals unopened.

Gerard Murphy

The Last Days in the History of Love

Now that we are no longer swans
As in the old days and float
Down the long lake of life together,
Now that the need for self-fulfilment
Is deemed a necessary end in itself
And selfishness an ambition to be pursued
As if it were some higher calling,

What will become of our children?
Those latch key interlopers
To our half-deserted homes.
These strangers with their even stranger
Needs, who we find, unexpectedly
Squatting on our lives like exotic
Birds come in from the cold?

Will they be damaged by this multiplicity
Of lives, this profusion of parents,
Half-hating, half-tolerating each other?
Will they be broken and scared
By layers and layers of bitterness
As other people's needs
Take precedence over theirs?

Or will they be in some way enriched
By this flux of change, this sportscar-like
Increase in the emotional mutation rate?
I am inclined to believe that some
May benefit and, when they grow
Older, create a whole raft of glum
Novels out of this dysfunctional freight.

While the others; the sensitive,
The vulnerable, the meek, will fall between
The cracks of their disjointed lives,
For the damage that adults wreak
Is high as clouds, dogfights in the sky,
Way up, exalted above the basement
Necessities of the lives of children,

And statistics too will rise, like Leviathans,
And the figures will show an increase
In all the usual signs; drug addiction,
Suicide, the standard afflictions
Of those for whom the floor of childhood
Is no floor at all, just an open field
Of conflict, a bewilderment of loss.

This is the new war, these are the new
Refugees; our children needing nurture.
For the dry lands of our brightened
Selfishness are too much of a desert
For giving the only things that we must give:
Support and nurture and the frightened
Creature that used to be known as love.

David Meagher

Brazilians
i.m. Aidan McAnespie

Brazilians, every one of us.

How we dazzled daily in the gleam
Of that Tyrone back yard –
A school of excellence where
Carlos Alberto, Zico, and a handful of Peles
Found fable in the grind.

A battered barn door marked
the sharpening of our craft –
Six-all, ten-nine, winning goals in extra-time:
where in the swivel and feint, mediocrity
couldn't touch our heels for dust.

Home from home with legend,
We spilled our separate ways, each
With Edson Arantes do Nascimento
As the measure of our reach.

Carolyn Jess

Postcards

Milk-marble full moon:
a camera shutter taking
photos for Heaven.

Rococo-gold leaves
melt from Fermanagh's boughs and
sail to new seasons.

Snow topping the Mournes
keeps cold footprints of last night
as sad souvenirs.

Whitsunday's white sands
are huddled bodies hiding
under the covers.

Auckland's blue tower
threads the Southern cross to north
and knits night's distance.

Sugarcane burning
over Fiji glows like fruit
on ocean's dark tree.

Glencar waterfall
drums nature's sonatina
on quiet black stones.

Tommy Curran

Venus at Home

but mostly I look at her
though through the window
you can see the garden's descent

from my armchair seat
the cul-de-sac ending road
then the green proximity

derelict fields, disused ground
overgrazed by the handful
of traveller-piebalds tethered

by long ropes and spaced out
across its slowfall
to the stepping parallels

main road then railway
that linear embankment
skirting for the marbled sky's

multiple of grey, diffusing
all shadow outdoors and in
giving muted colour

and to her red and blue
she pre-dressed in dressing gown
and pajama, orbiter

of her own space
reclining on the couch, her head
propped by her left forearm

she is looking askew at some
sunday morning tv drama
talk illumined images

switch and flick
aside the centre spectrum
her burgundy coloured toenails

Aimée Sands

The League of the One-Breasted Women

I was hugged by two one-breasted women
last night in spitfire dark, in matte cold
who marked my face as
someone lost, and fastened
one breast each
on each of my shoulders.
I have been anointed.

Two breasts one breast sound breast
whole breast what
is the weight of a breast lifted
and released, the fine skin
laid on the beating heart?
There are different ways
you know you're there.
When you are hugged
by a one-breasted woman
you are her other breast
pressed to the rib skin
that still remembers the breasted weight
the breasted child that flew.

I was hugged by two
one-breasted women last night
and inside their coats
one breast lay flat
the other was a wing.
And the breast that lived
spoke to me in a feather voice
spoke to me in a liver voice
counted my two breasts
whispered saints' code to each
and turned over; then each
one-breasted woman patted
her lone breast, offered me one,
kept the other.

Gary Allen

Bethlehem down

I was born with no roof in my mouth:
a hysterical girl found despair
in the black openness,

who ran screaming to the streets,
He is not right.

Damned infants have only themselves to blame:

the sudden presence that sends goat herds
panicking down scree:

slit throats in Judea:

babies thrown by burning mothers
pitchforked back into the flames:

small lungs exploding on poisoned air.

The sirens of the mills speak for me
the tongues of smoke is my taste

my cradle is history –
the prophecy in the stony desert come to pass,

the humpback, the club-foot,
the bloody embryo in the broken egg.

Moya Cannon

Walking out to Islandeddy

Sometimes, at low spring tide in February,
if the wind is right,
the moon hauls the sea back off the sand bar
for an hour or two.

We have stumbled down over wrack-draped stones
and have waited as, quickly, yard by yard
it rises out of the tide—
an arm of sand
which holds an island of roofless houses
to the shore.

Unwilling to wait
for the sea to part completely
we wade the first few yards,
and come up onto a highway
of rough gold and black sand and purple scallop fans.
Sarah says "This is how the Israelites crossed the Red Sea.
They must have known the tides well."

Behind us, a man and his grown son have been driving
a flock of black-faced sheep along the grassline.
Now they head them down the shore
through salty pools, wrack and kelp.
Reaching the edge,
one sheep is manhandled through the last few feet of water.
The others scatter, bleating,
but are gathered and herded over
onto their sea road.

We have to stand back as they pass,
their small hooves crushing and crushing loudly into the seabed.
Scenting their summer grass,
they start to speed up and trot
between the upright flutes of razor shells
and the tiny, breath-driven geysers of the clams.

Joan McBreen

Knockma in Spring

Late February snow in the fields
and the Corrib a ribbon of silver
in the distance. We climb Knockma,
stopping for breath after each of the five
inclines, time and again being surprised
by the slender branches of birches, white
as girls in Communion dresses. Mulch
of dead leaves under our feet
and the velvet silence at last
when we reach the summit. A catch
in the throat, eyes smarting in the cold,
and the words we share are echoes
astonishing us in a world
that is suddenly hidden or half-seen.

Nessa O'Mahony

To my dear biographer
from Mary Wollstonecraft to William Godwin

No man knew me better, or treated me
more as equal in heart and intellect.
We forged our own society, late, it's true,
and would have endured after all the false beginnings,
the moments when an end seemed
the only outcome to my Werther wanderings.

I chose death, but death, it seems,
could bide its time. Till then,
you were the bridge where I could leap
to the depths of an untroubled sleep,
a waking up to warmth. The golden age
that lasted eighteen months.

Did you forget, then, in those first
few weeks, shutting out the world,
poring over drafts, food trays piling up,
pausing only to refill a glass,
sharpen the tallow wick,
as the ink flowed, word upon word?

Didn't you recall the Tønsberg church,
the dusty crypt where life
was petrified into remembrance?
Treasons against humanity, I said.
Did you really want my corpse preserved,
my sins etched out on the embalmer's plate?

Art Murphy

Lachrymae Rerum

Sleep was pushed from its ledge
when the children appeared
at our bedroom door and said
the rabbit's yelp had wakened them.
We ran to the garden pen
and saw scratched earth beneath the mesh.

Fur hung on wire like votive rags.
They looked for the rabbit everywhere
but all they saw were starlings
forage in slug-black litter
and grey mushroom spores scatter
into mist. What grieved me most

was that a cracked rowan's ooze
glazed their trailing hands
and that they could not see
the veins that pencilled their skin
as intricate and foreign
as specimen leaves under glass.

Art Murphy

Elsewhere

Was there ever a time
when dreams and visions
did not start in dried things

in husks or shells or stones
scraps of the world
lying about us

in sunlight on a wall
and butterfly wings pulsing
in that pool of silence?

Or in hooded Spring –
as the elsewhere
of the heart?

The sweet mercy
of looking there
instead of everywhere.

William Oxley

No Real Present

It's all a sort of memory,
the good times, the bad –
that perfect meal
oysters, steak, wines of France
like the Marne in sunlight,
lovers in each others' eyes –
always memories.

Today we were in a green village
cows on the easy valley's side
a low-slung inn
the white sky world –
some other mind maybe.

The few convivial hours that pass
their tragic shortness long-felt,
that only art's striving can capture –
there is no real present
only history, mystery, memory.

The present is a slipping away
and all we have is memory
of what or who
is other than ourselves –
the colourfall of fuchsias
in a July garden,
every man and woman going home
elsewhere to some other life

a life not known or seen
like wind, but remembered
sure as touch.

William Oxley

The South Country

'There is no great poetry which can be dissevered from Nature'
— Edward Thomas

The Barley Mow, a pub
on the spruced up banks of Thames,
once a Custom's House
now it bears this rural name.
But the Thames here is wide,

wide as a poet's heart; and the river
smell is a sea smell. Clay-
coloured waters, seasoned with salt,
that chuckle in stones and mud.

Nearby the Isle of Dogs is a new
Little City: huge phials of glass
filled with specimen humans
obliterating waste land and wharf.
And Limehouse, too, is themed and clean.

The frozen drama of the post-modern
surrounds me.

            This South Country is changed.
Ineluctably, like a make-over of God.

George Evans

Girls in the Trees

The onus is upon us to believe in nothing,
and that religion, like all religions,

happens with great force until understood
to be one further thing between us and the world.

But on this day in Montana, two young girls
riding bareback through a Quaking Aspen stand

– fists knotted into fiery black manes, they run
their giants through blurring, gold shaking trees –

are every reason to believe nothing but what we see,
until what we see erases what we believe.

Eamon Grennan

Mid-May's Eldest Child

How they keep themselves to themselves, invisible among the high branches
Leafing after a week of rain and fattening to greenness – these nests in which
The earnest householders have begun again their cycle of song, hunger, song –
The only evidence of them this noose of urgent notes they fling about us
And the speckled or turquoise shells cracked empty at our feet each morning.
How the whole place is, in a week, shrouded in green; how the Canada geese
Have four families of nibblers by the lake; how the dogwood has grown plush
In its rich pinks and altar-whites; how apple blossom, cherry blossom and
The flowers of whitethorn have all withered; how the grass has become a lush
Green rug in which dusklight keeps gleaming: how *again* it is, and happening.

Gerard Beirne

Properties of Solutions: The Colloidal State

take atoms, molecules
assume their use theoretically
if not practically
believe in them (or not)
if you will

accept (for now) that this
is elementary theory
to avoid a state of confusion

focus on colloidal dispersion
the scattering of light (for instance)
by particles of dust
in the path of a sunbeam
through a partly opened door
(call this the *Tyndell effect*)

take these small sparkling specks
(these giant steps)
and follow these points of reflected light
observe the constant random motion
(name it *Brownian movement*)

publish if you must
a mathematical analysis
of non-uniform random collisions
caused by the unequal number of molecules
colliding on either side

(answer if you dare
to the name of Einstein

or Perrin if you prefer,
a Nobel Prize)

verify experimentally
remove the last doubts surrounding
atoms and molecules, offer
the proof of your own existence

(act surprised)

the notion of its constant
random motion
the human condition

believe in it (or not)
if you will

(but accept for now
that this is still

elementary
          theory)

Eugenio Montale

The Mirages*

Not always or almost never does our personal identity
      coincide
with time measurable with the instruments we have.
The room is big, it has friezes and baroque stuccos,
and the large back window reveals a golden park of Styria,
with some wisps of mist the sun is dissolving.
The interior is pure Vermeer, smaller and more realistic
than reality but with an incorruptible enamel.
On the left, a young girl dressed as a page,
all lace and fine embroidery down to her knee,
is playing with her beloved little monkey.
On the right, her older sister, Arabella,
is consulting a black fortune-teller
who is revealing the impending future to her.
A man of noble lineage is about to join them,
the invincible hero she was waiting for.
It is a question of little time, of minutes, seconds,
soon the stamping of his horses' hooves will be heard
and then someone will knock at the door...
                                                              but
here my eye tires and withdraws itself
from the keyhole. I have already seen too much
and the temporal ribbon is rewinding itself.
Whoever has worked the miracle is a beer-soaked sponge,
or so he seems, and his companion is the last
Knight Errant of Christianity.

. . . . . .

but now
if I re-read myself I think that only anonymity
rules the world, creates it and destroys it
so as to forever re-fashion it more ghost-like
and unrecognisable. There remains the peep-hole
of the almost photographic painter to warn us
that if something once was there is no distance
between the millennium and an instant, between who
appeared and did not appear, between who lived
and he who did not achieve focus of his spyglass. It is
not much and, perhaps it is all.

– translated by Giovanni Malito

* 'I miraggi' is the second last poem in Montale's sixth collection, *Quaderno di quattro anni* (1977), and is a typical example of his later poetry. The poem is centred on a dreamlike vision – featuring the characters from the opera *Arabella*, music by Richard Strauss and libretto by Hugo von Hofmannsthal – which provides the poet with the platform for another of his existential 'roundabouts'.

Ann Killough

The Birdfeeder

It hangs there like a heart, my heart.
Soft bodies flutter against it and the shadows of leaves,
the sharp pecking, inside.

It feels like some kind of acknowledgement,
some accession to knowledge, to extension;
it feels like submission,

of course, but there's also a verticality,
like a raised arm.
Yesterday afternoon, late, when the mourning doves came,

two of them, with their long speckled wings
and their calm heads, and fed, one at a time,
the other one waiting, the smaller birds waiting,

the sky fading to pale –
I wasn't sure I wanted something so big
knocking against my heart,

despite the low morning call, hollow and grievous,
or maybe because of it –
I wasn't sure I could accommodate the size,

the breast, like a softening fruit.
Later, in the dark, when I came back to water the plants,
I was glad to see nothing there,

the feeder alone, swinging a little,
insouciantly, as though abandoned at last.
Today the sparrows were back,

alert and famished, with that partitive quality,
as if each were a crumb of the loaf,
of a brown loaf, powdery and plain,

as if each were a drop of something,
blood from a casual wound,
small but unmistakable, that would leave a scar –

I'm not sure what it is I want to know,
except whether they really need it,
whether they couldn't find nourishment elsewhere,

and should –
whether all this untidy labour and repetition
is really required, despite the pleasures of it,

the adventure and return, the bright eyes blinking –
if it's worth it, remaking holiness,
if that's what it is,

letting it accrete again, like this,
event by event, letting it be about
feeding, and depletion, about flocking together

in a swirl of hungers –
about the hanging body,
again, incessant wings.

Ivy Bannister

Appetite

These lords and ladies expect quails and quince in sugar,
but all they do is grouse: "This swan is too dry;
its sauce stinks of fish;" then they rag me till I cry.

I flee in dudgeon to my cook-house, bowel-deep
in their marble-pillared manor, cut off from fields
of lavender that stretch towards a teal-blue sea;

only something's astir: a shudder of foundations;
a heaving breeze that flaps mighty galleons.
I listen, scheme, pick at the wart on my thumb.

Don't I know the workings of borage, nettles and cabbage?
Of black bile and porous pans of lead? For,
when night falls, am I not a creature too?

I take on *nouvelle cuisine,* shape dainty morsels
with crimping fingers, geometric fantasies of
leaf, fowl and fungus. Too pretty to eat,

but these lords and lassies can't get enough.
Snuffling like piggi-wigs, they laud me to the skies.
My laugh is a wind-chime; my lips are a plum.

Spring has come. Now I feed myself alone,
nothing flash, just figs and sprouts.
In the afternoons I stroll by the sea, collect shells,

whistle,
dance
in the lavender wind.

Alice Lyons

The Polish Language
– for Barbara Falkowska and her family

If language could shrug shoulders
lift eyebrows and turn palms up
you might have a tiny idea.

To make an effigy, you'd need
a lot of concrete, more than you'd think
a stork, some amber
honey from bees that live near rape
a quantity of shirts freely removed
from the backs of anyone you meet
big lumps of lead and coal
and a great deal of wood from a primeval forest.

A poultice of sliced onions on the throat
may help you speak it.

Cats are known to rub up against its sibilance.

Crush a cherry and a beet
in your fingers to arrive at its colour –
czerwony.
If that fails to convince, make a soup.

When you are fed up with the world,
say *sprzykrzy*
or phone information in Zakopane
and just listen.

As a matter of fact
in this sonorous consonant tongue
my art was revivified.

My Polish brothers and sisters
in art (the ones who survived)
robbed of flint you made fire
out of evil you wrote *live*.

Rody Gorman

Dosán den Fheamainn Bhuí

Ní hé barrainneach
Gur shleamhnaigh tú uaim i do dhosán
Den fheamainn bhuí, díreach
Go raibh mé féin
Mar a bheadh cloch reatha ann,
Gan a bheith dílis ná daingean
Sa gcaoi
Nach bhfásfá féin uirthi.

Ealta Fearbóg

Cuimhne
Mar ealta fearbóg bíogtha le gal gan coinne
I mbéal na gaoithe
Ar a siúl oíche
Faoin ngarraí
Thíos ar bhéal an tí:

Clascairt. Priosarnaíl. Trostal cos faoin raon.
Ag rúchadh leo mar tháin
Agus – de phreabadh na súl –
Ar shiúl.

Annie Deppe

Night Voices

As they readied to leave, my father
reached into his suit coat pocket, brought out
a handful of coins. *For the radio...*

I lined up ten shiny dimes on the cotton sheet.
Above me, a radio mounted on the wall.
I was five, could count to over one hundred.

In the corner bed, a boy named Jimmy wailed.
Only four. *Cry baby*. This was before
they wheeled me into the dark brown room

and the bad mask clamped down over my nose.
Before backwards counting. That night
I lay waiting in the hospital's half-light,

slid one thin dime after another into the radio's slot.
The row grew shorter, and it suddenly
came to me – if I used the last coin,

they would never come back.
Of my mother, all I remembered
was her hair folded in a bun, and of my father

his speckled white hands. As I fell asleep
I heard their voices on radio, trying
to comfort me. A hundred miles away.

Daisy Zamora

Proposal

Now that we've come back
    from that dream
      we went on scattering
along a path we chose without
                knowing,
let's collect the pieces
    that shine in the depths
of memory like stars
        in deepest night.

    From splendour dispersed
let's put the fragments together as a lamp
    to illuminate our faces,
and light, at least, a small bonfire
    to shelter us against the wild.

              – translated by George Evans and Daisy Zamora

Bei Dao

Black Map

in the end, cold crows piece together
the night: a black map
I come back home – the way back
is always longer than the wrong road
long as all one's life

bring the heart of winter
when the spring water and the honey pills
become the words of night
when memory barks
the rainbow haunts the black market

my father's life-spark small as a pea
I am his echo
turning at the corner for encounters
the ex-lover hides in the wind
swirling with letters

Beijing, let me
toast your lamplights
let my white hair lead
the way through the black map
as though a storm were taking you to fly

I wait in line until the small window
is shut: O the bright moon
I come back home – reunions
are less than goodbyes
only one less

– translated by Eliot Weinberger

§ Poets and War §

Aileen Kelly

Documentary

All those grey ships aflame
ripped and dragged under
colours unstruck
and my father not on board
that one that one that one.
Worsening odds. All our future
life that circled round him
could have
sucked itself down.
Under the stairs under the planes
I babied asleep didn't
even worry.

Fifteen wide-awake I found
his middle-age hunched at the TV.
At academic comment
and German archive film.
Soundless the thump of gunnery
shuddered his back.
Numbering down the crews.
Naming.

Each night (I suppose
now there's only me to dream
his silent history)
his friends walked the undersea
terrain from which no bubbles rise.
They carry their dead his dead each
other in disintegrated arms.

Fred Johnston

War Poem for the Anxious
– for Eoin Dubsky

When he decides to kill
He'll sight the enemy, wait
For orders –

Down the technological
Marvel of the barrel, the
Snug stock under the arm:

It's night-goggles
And a green world, like
Being underwater, drowning.

Susan Wicks

Christmas
*from eye-witness accounts of the Great War,
in Flanders Fields Museum, Cloth Hall, Ieper*

Stille Nacht: men's voices rise
from the trenches. In your sights
a man staggers with a fir-tree
and you don't shoot –
you watch the small star travel
and come to rest – a stable,
a child bedded in straw
where the warm animals still are.
And men are leaving their watches
for a kick-out in No-Man's-Land,
snipping through wet cotton
with wire-cutters, trading buttons.
Time stops. Time to repair
your cat's-cradle of barbed wire,
bring in your stiffened dead.
You've come so far
with beer, tobacco, oranges:
no wonder you hardly draw breath
there, on the bank at Diksmuide,
feeling the rope vibrate
as the host glides towards you
over the frozen river,
in its rime-bag of cloth.

Danny Hardisty

The Airman

How to grasp hands with the world when I can't
remember myself? The cord brings the staff
from their different shifts. You chance your arm for
who you get; *nobody* at half past three.
My window looks to a squarish garden. An
open ledge allows a taste of the sun.

I can go back four decades, but not days.
July the Twenty-Sixth Nineteen-Forty –
my 'seventeenth', a brother at twenty.
I lied my way past certificates, forms;
like talking a woman up sweetly. Then dawn:
blear-eyed Heidelberg and Frankfurt
fourteen months the wiser, and me drawing
rear-gunner, the butt of the craft. Cracks, storms –
the anti-aircraft measuring a hand
ahead of your nose, and hitting your tail.
The sight of Lancasters tipping from the sky
like fairground carriages. My heart had failed.

We bombed Dresden six of seven, returning
time over. Its family photograph curled,
down below me – upturned edges burning.
The heat enough to warm my frozen cheeks.
The strange half and half of dawn, part the world
open as an eye, and part blackest sky.

Don't misunderstand, I've had life between:
one family, then a second, and grandchildren.
None of us any different from the rest,
lucky to be alive, but the *real* luck –
its high pitch whistle, and then its pause,
checking the pulse of life to find yourself
still here; the luck that drags on through months –
not chance, or prayers, or those other stores.
By rights I don't deserve even this bed.

Ten years ago I walked my granddaughter
through the park at Wibsey, a burnt-out car
sat in the boating lake. We had done for
cities, railways, streets, factories as grim as those
left back behind us over the water.
I sit in my chair, as I am supposed –
now ill enough for a second divorce.
Senility, drink, each thing has its cause.
I do not expect visits having hidden
myself to myself through two marriages.
Besides whose face do I really know now?
Memory burns out its own fires. 'I kept
quiet long enough for no-one to listen.'

Patrick Cotter

Letter to Charles Simic, April 1999
When power corrupts, poetry cleanses
      – John F Kennedy, November 1962

Days spirited past like a monitor's flicker.
All the while a heavy cable, slotted
into the serial port jutting from my neck,
had gone undetected by my left-hand cerebrum.

But the right side of my brain, eager to
display its smart-aleck capacity for plug-and-play,
related at breakfast how this connection alone
powered all NATO bombing in Serbia.

On television I saw a man use his severed leg
as a crutch and a boy feed his pet dog
his own shock-blasted German Shepherd eyes:
substitutes for embargoed *Pedigree Yum*.

In a fit of judicious revulsion
I ripped the cable away.
Immediately Americans started to fall
from the skies like fucked-out ant drones.

Sky News beamed pictures of
mid-West mammies moaning.
Shreds of yellow ribbons flickered
from blue-rinse locks like plaintive snow.

Before anyone could notice
and choose to erase *my* children
I tried to reconnect the wires
as if they were as simple

as the TV serial bombarding me
with simplistic coverage all week;
but the filaments were too complex
the connectors too multitudinous.

After my efforts,
B52s flew upside down
Pershing missiles cruised backwards
like show-off sparrowhawks on E.

Fergus Allen

On Wexford Bridge
– i.m. JH Colclough

I

When I was a small boy my relatives
Had a skeleton in their mental cupboard
That was not referred to except
Through slips of the tongue at mealtimes,
And these incurred frowns of reproof.

When brain death overcame these elders
The skeleton had to move house
And, finding himself in the sunlight,
Surprised us all when he was greeted
Right and left as a martyred patriot.

Death by hanging could now be mentioned,
Even boasted of, as though virtue
Could be gained by association –
We had genes in common with 'A Leader
Of Seventeen Ninety-Eight'.

II

I, John Henry Colclough, am the subject
Of those attention-seeking stanzas.
But it's for me, now in my timelessness,
To reflect on those dreadful months
When we were chewed up and disgorged.

We were 'three respectable gentlemen
Of the County of Wexford', Edward
Fitzgerald, Beauchamp Bagenal Harvey
And myself (a qualified physician),
All landowners in a modest way

And 'men of liberal principles',
Troubled by injustices inflicted
On our neighbours – townsfolk, small farmers,
Their hired hands, most of them Catholic,
But God's creatures for all that –

And terrified of the bands of Orangemen,
The bigots with their so-called loyalty
To the unloved couple from Holland.
In their eyes Papists' bodies looked well
On gallows and roadside gibbets;

Tolerance was midwife to treason.
Many events were veiled by storms
And whirlwinds were whisked up by passion,
Veering unpredictably here
And there with their acts of undoing.

III

Seventeen ninety-eight, and the Quakers
Were founding their school in Waterford,
But most minds were on the Orange devils,
Ravaging the townlands for provender
And the subjugation of idolaters.

The military were in tumult,
Coming and going and saving their skins
At the cost of firearms and howitzers
Lost to the insurrectionists.
General Fawcett scurried back

To the grey fortress in Duncannon,
Having lost his men and matériel
At the rebel-held Three Rocks,
Which caused Colonel Maxwell to feel shame
But pull his own men back to Wexford.

The Donegal militia hanged
Four prisoners in Clonegall,
Though the gentlemen of the town
Spoke up for them as loyal citizens.
That took Lieutenant Young, the Duty

Officer, two hours to accomplish.
Under a soft blue sky, with cloudlets
Drifting peacefully across from Clare,
Pigs were observed in Gorey's streets
To eat the bodies of insurgents

Recently shot, some still expiring.
And while a soft wind brushed his cheek
A soldier fired into a bush,
Dragged out a screaming boy of eight,
Six other children and their mother.

Hearing of this my wife cried aloud
And my children, knowing they were weak
And scared by such uncensored feelings,
Slipped away to the back of the paddock
To a hiding-place in the ha-ha.

Rumours flickered like summer lightning,
Wild crowds streamed into market places,
Howling and drunk on looted spirits;
There was no rule and no safe keeping,
The cabins' thatch went up in flames.

Heroics, glamour and romance
Were, as always, the absentee darlings;
In truth, on all sides, chaos and savagery
(Called manliness by misanthropes),
Wound up in unbridled cruelty.

IV

But the red cows had to be milked
And the mushrooms went on growing
In the long green grass, where the horses
(Or those that had not been stolen),
Still stood around flicking their tails.

The dung-flies went about their business
In the shade of the hawthorn hedges,
Unaware of the rage and fear
That poisoned the last week of May
And evacuated many bowels.

V

From information received and
On the 'suspicion of treasonable
Designs', a Captain Boyd arrested
Harvey, Fitzgerald and myself;
And threw us into Wexford prison.

What information? From what source?
This was not revealed, but ill-will
And slander is the likely answer.
We had not hidden our contempt
For all harsh upstart Orangemen.

But under pressure at the drumhead
Edward Fitzgerald and myself,
Though forbidden to offer terms,
Agreed to ride to Enniscorthy
To parley with the mutinous crowd

And urge them back to their homes.
It was an anxious day of riding
Through mist and challenges and threats,
But when we fetched up at Vinegar Hill
The crowd, though restless and distracted

And at cross purposes among themselves,
Agreed to hear me out in silence;
When I had said my say the rebels
Disputed at the tops of their voices,
Mixing arguments and abuse

Like oil and kindling, with the hotheads
Throwing the last word, the flaming match.
Somehow through all that argy-bargy
They resolved to march at once on Wexford –
But to detain my friend Fitzgerald.

Back in Wexford's bull ring, on horseback,
I, playing Stentor, owned our failure
To sway the will of the insurgents –
Soon to arrive with pikes and forks.
Then in fulfilment of my promise

I took Bagenal Harvey's place in gaol.
There followed frenzy and confusion,
The town stormed and plundered, fired,
All prisoners released, green boughs
Hung up as emblems of insurgency,

Fleeing troops massacring the peasants –
Suffering that cannot be thought of
(And in those days no one spoke of rape).
But when retaken by the military,
The principal citizens were gaoled

And formally arraigned for treason.
Harvey, myself and our true wives
Fled by boat to the Saltee Islands,
Hoping to weather out the storms
Of that fearful time in a cave.

But Protestant cleanliness betrayed us
When laundry laid out on the rocks
By our particular spouses
Was spotted from a passing cutter
And a message passed post-haste to Wexford.

So we were discovered and brought back,
Watched by a crowd on Kilmore Quay,
Whence we two men were led to gaol
And the condemned cells, to await
Court martial and its foregone ending.

Traitors, found guilty of commitment
To the abolition of bigotry
Through the arm of the United Irishmen,
We and the others were condemned.
Harvey was hanged on Wexford Bridge,

His body stripped and treated
'With the usual brutal indecencies'
(Words that mean 'hanged, drawn and quartered')
And his head transfixed on a pike.
Then I, after incontinent panic

And that most terrible paroxysm,
Looked down and saw myself
Hanging from a scaffold on the bridge.
(Smile if you will, but I wish to say
That as a gentleman I'd been allowed

To wear my coat during the ritual).
At the pleading of my dearest wife
I saw my corpse delivered up to her,
Laid out and taken away by cart
To Ballyteigue for decent burial.

Others that day – Grogan, Kelly, Keogh –
Died under even greater savagery.
Fitzgerald, though, became a leader
At Vinegar Hill, fought and surrendered
And lived to end his days in Hamburg.

VI

As always is the way
The players knew their parts
But could not see the play;

And neither brains nor hearts
Yesterday or today
Can explicate the kinds
Of fissures that ran through
The crystals of the minds
And eyes of those that slew.
Hate ulcerates and blinds.

VII

1922, early evening:
Miss Colclough sits in the drawing-room
Of her house, built into the ruins
Of Tintern Abbey, Wexford. What-nots
In mother-of-pearl, and Union flags;

Miss Colclough's skirts trail on the floor,
A modesty vest conceals her poverty.
Knock on the door, to which she goes,
Opens and sees the skyline lit
By flames from burning country houses.

An open car parked on the gravel,
Men in the trench coats of convention,
The IRA of course. 'Miss Colclough,
We know of that fine man, your cousin,
John Henry Colclough – have no fear,

Your home will be spared, you may sleep
And dream of an Ireland being born.'
And so it was. My father snapped her
In 1933, the Union flag
Still aloft in the drawing-room –

A mild old lady in a tea gown,
Keeping up her strange appearances,
Having made a truce with a past
That it was painful to think about
But painful to think of forgetting.

Kieran Furey

How Rome Rises as it Ruins
after Virgil

Forgive me this: that when I sleep I dream
of Harpies, Strophades and Hecatombs;
of Roman wars all Greek to me; of bombs
that fall from skies on mountains, caves and chasms.

And in such dreams I see whole landscapes burn
as *once again the ravenous birds return,*
from the dark recesses where they lie
or from another quarter of the sky.

And in my dreams the Harpies are not fed
enough to make them stop. No, they are led
by huge and ugly hungers to seek out
more food wherever they can find a threat.

Michael Brophy

View from the Gun

The pit of the V
Is centred on the dot
Of metal
That is my sight
Which is centred on the dot
Of flesh
That is his head.

I breathe and exhale
And as the air leaves
My lungs
The bullet leaves
My gun
To take the breath
From his life.

Another casualty for the columns
Another point for our performance,
Only by our score
Do they judge us,
Only when we are strong
Will they talk with us.

Peace is our purpose.

Leland Bardwell

The Invisible from Iraq to the USA

I am too late again
I have to get my bearings
In the gutter

The sky is dark,
The birds assemble –
A murder of crows

I dream of justice
Where a pride of lawyers
Tumbles through my brain

I must take action, I say
Against the invisible
It thinks it has me trapped

It likes to throw pipebombs
At unsuspecting babies
As it shouts out loudly
"She's only a girl-woman
Crying on the sofa"

Fred Marchant

ars poetica
  – for Ted Sexauer, in Baghdad

while poetry,
it is salt from a mine in Thessalonika,
or from the inland seas of California
that will break

underfoot into
pellets to melt the plated ice and cling
to the legislative shoe and trouser,
thereby eating

as if the flesh
were in the end actually the soul and the bone
inside just a conscience that sooner or later
would be reached

even though
the tongue that curious extension of flesh
on the butcher's block would swear in court
if it could talk

that our salts
taste more like the iodines of blood,
or the copper of spit, and have nothing
to do with tears

Fred Marchant

Collateral

Someone at the source said it would
be impossible for you to be.

When you took it in, it coloured you
in coppery sorrow. You turned

your head away and held yourself
down, pressed that flimsy little

European suit against the earth
as if beneath was a great river

where at one end it was early morning,
and at the other, just night.

The Shelter

As if the light were not a storm targeting you.
As if in the hollow you could hide, or wait it out.
As if you would not be drained of everything red in your body.
As if you could hold your breath the entire time.
As if you thought you were safe and not lying.

T Michael Sullivan

First Snow

Driven out by spring's dance and exiled
from memory long ago, the flakes

lingered first at the fence
and tucked around the posts.

They piggybacked the lawn
and steps and picnic table

while talk of war rode a bucking
wind, and words of peace

wandered, like new refugees
clutching hope, now a scant

possession, in search of a thin strip
of land to settle and seed.

Kevin Bowen

The Post-Nuclear Age
– for Jonathan Schell

My friend tells me he thanks God
each morning when he wakes up
to find the world still there outside
his window. He goes to sleep
counting warheads. He cannot count
sheep for they are too close to the truth
of us, he says, for we have all fallen
into an amnesia, he swears, forgotten
how the bombs lie still buried at
the bottoms of the silos & submerged
in dark boats at the bottom of the hundred
seas. One for each man, woman, and child
in a good-sized city. Enough to blow
the earth up a few thousand times.
And yet we keep making more, needing
then to think up new names for them,
like the bunker-busting bomb,
designed for deeper penetration,
and then there are the ones we'll send
into space. It almost seems funny,
but he knows better and so hardly sleeps.
There are others like him who pace
unable to sleep & move unseen through
the night. Like those three nuns who
broke through the fences of the bases
in Colorado, dressed in outfits
like spacemen. When caught they
said they were weapons inspectors,
out searching for Weapons of Mass Destruction.
They poured blood on the silos' lids:
Sister Anne Montgomery, 75, Order
of the Sacred Heart; Sisters Ardeth Platte, 66,
Jackie Hudson, 67, Dominicans both.
They beat on the lids with their handcuffs
again and again, before being dragged away.

John F Deane

The Aftertaste of Bitterness

The roof slopes steeply;
I am listening to Bach, the St John Passion: *I live,
the pleasures of love enjoying, and thou
art dying*. How the attic space
has grown luxurious with the music, oboe

d'amore, a thunder-storm, a dulcet
rending of the heart in sorrow; and I fill,
if only for a moment, with
transcendental energy. Clouds
through the skylight window shift, reform,

there falls a huge knocking on the glass
from the opened sky. Peter's
ham-fisted effort at violence, the swung
sword; then the music of healing, the forgiving
hand. *And what is truth?* I'm drawn away

by mating-shouts of pheasants
in the high grass outside. Bach's slow chorales
lift the soul, through time, out
beyond time, till the music tells how death
is the perfect state of innocence.

*

Truth is this: the weak
pitch themselves bodily against might; violence,
the swung
sword, comes with un-

anticipated speed, and dwells
in the slow absurdity of dream; this
is truth: jagged-edged girders shape a cross
that has taken root where stone

burned down to ash. Still
burning. It will be difficult
to look to the sky again with confidence. Under
temporary hoardings a down-and-almost-out

was playing the flute-music of affliction; where, it sang,
am I to go from here? Humanity, alone in the universe, has learned
how to hate. What are the uses
of poetry? and its responsibilities? Imagine

the smaller things: a kitsch glass paperweight
on a desk, a man's
fingers fidgeting with it; a tall
girl walking across a hallway for a glass of chilled

water; and how it took so long (split
seconds) to see what it was that was pitching itself
bodily against them: the
future, and its sudden lack, and how the glass

melted instantly, the fingers with it, how the water
scalded suddenly, the tall girl
with it; and countless other
instances: the stuff of gravity; and finally how the distance

between us and God is
death. I listened to the patient
whine of air-conditioning in my hotel room; a man
in Washington Square performed

the dream-like Tao dance; leaves on the trees
have shaken themselves free
of dust; streets are decked out again
in the decorum of commerce. Affliction

leaves an aftertaste of bitterness, like sloe-juice
cramping the tongue; and nowhere can you hear
the poem of *Father, forgive them*; it is might, seeking
to be mightier. I dressed

in my blue shirt, my priest-black
trousers, settled my papers to performance mode,
sought weighted words, to say to the hopeless *hope*
to the unforgiven *mercy*, my tongue

was swollen in my mouth, language
needing to start over. I set out
down the indifferent streets to where I must speak:
Sometimes, in impossible places. . .

Rita Ann Higgins

Grandchildren

It's just not feasible at the moment
one daughter tells me.
What with Seamus still robbing banks
and ramming garda vans when he gets emotional
on a fish free Friday in February.

Maybe the other daughter could deliver.
She thinks not, not at the moment anyway
while Tomás still has a few tattoos to get
to cover any remaining signs that might link him
to the rest of us.

Just now a B52 bomber flies over
on its way to Shannon
to make a gulf in some nation's genealogy.

The shadow it places on all our notions is crystal clear
and for a split of a second helping
it juxtaposes the pecking order,
now bank robbers and tattooers
have as much or as little standing
as popes and princes
and grandchildren become another lonely utterance
impossible to pronounce.

Ger Killeen

Sometimes Instead of a Poem

It is 8a.m. I am
grinding coffee beans in
the kitchen. Water

is beginning to boil
in the copper-bottomed kettle
and kindling is snapping

in the woodstove.
The cat sidles out
of the coat-closet

as the smell steams up
from a pan of bacon. Outside
the sky is trying to snow.

Where you get to
saying these things
is neither here nor there:

There may never be a song
that puts the pieces
together, but say them

anyway. Say them when
the war comes to suck at
your life; when they jail you

for being too human, say them;
pray them at the bishops
blessing the missiles;

and whisper them
to your lover
in the dark of the night

instead of a poem. Say them
to remember the ecstasies
of dailiness,

the fact of a world
there and graspable
in pots and pans;

say them before you stop
believing that paradise is
pulsing under our fingers.

Mary Branley

Wait for me
– for Paddy, Charlie and Brian

Momma stand at the door
where the sun goes down
and wait for me

I can manage by myself,
When I'm tired I suck my thumb,
I can feel my time is near
And I'm afraid of what's in store

Momma stand at the door
Where the sun goes down
And wait for me

I can pee now just like Dad.
And I don't need you anymore
But at times I get confused
I'm afraid I'll wet my pants

Momma stand at the door
Where the sun goes down
And wait for me

I go to school with the other boys
And I learn my lessons well
I bite my lip when I want to cry
And I cover up my fears

Momma stand at the door
Where the sun goes down
And wait for me

I'm away to the city now
First to college, then a job
It's not easy on your own
I can't say that I miss home

Momma stand at the door
Where the sun goes down
And wait for me

My first child's just been born
And my wife and I are tired
Who'll look after the little ones
When they send me off to war?

Momma stand at the door
Where sun goes down
And wait for me

We play cards to pass the time
While we're waiting for the word
No-one tells us what's going on
The night gets freezing cold

Momma stand at the door
Where the sun goes down
And wait for me.

Ciaran O'Driscoll

A Gift for the President
*"Mr Bush's appearance today to receive a bowl of shamrock
from the Taoiseach, Mr Ahern, at the White House..."*
– The Irish Times, *13 March 2003*

I hold seminars on this sort of thing.
'Why,' I ask my art students,
'is there a bunch of bananas beside
the female torso in de Chirico's
The Uncertainty of the Poet?'
And one student says,
'This is presumably the poet
uncertain how she can eat a banana
without a hand to pick it up,
or a mouth to put it in.'

The problem with Surrealism
is how much more surreal it can get
the more you tease it out,
therefore those art commentators
are wise who remain deadpan:
'What we really have here,' I say,
'is the unexpected juxtaposition
of a twisted classical female torso
and a big bunch of bananas.'

And another student asks:
'Why are there trains in the background?'

'De Chirico always has trains in the background.
It's kind of his signature.'

The other problem with Surrealism
is that it's not confined to art.
'Why,' I ask, 'is there a big bunch
of shamrock in the Taoiseach's bowl?'

And a promising student says:
'This is the unexpected juxtaposition
of a bellicose American President
and a bowl of shamrock in the hands
of an abject Irish Prime Minister.
Here the classical and renaissance sense
of calm, balance and harmony
is distorted to make the scene
more sinister and disturbing.'

'Good, good, very good, excellent!
And why are there planes in the background?'

'The President always has planes in the background.
It's kind of his signature.'

Medbh McGuckian

Picasso's Windows

If the war lengthens,
It claws the zones
And kneads the built-up area
Of the boy's head, for a month-or-so;

If body enters body,
We are invited to rearrange the stars,
The heavenscape of starsouls,
With hard patches of sound,

All the waters the earth could not suffer
In its smallest veins.
Nothing has ever flown
Through this dresdenized air before,

Not even a fallen angel
Lying soulless, tearing his eyes away
From his blue martyrdom,
Which leaves an eye nestling

In his two islands of hair,
And encourages the eye to rest there.
Almost exactly a year later,
The charcoaled azure, as if rubbed with ashes,

Tracks every breath
Of that heavy dose of blue
Wherein he once made shadow.
With a hand he knows,

Outstretched as a shade
Of red pearls that never depart from circling,
He muffles his underlying colours
And the lilac of his arms

In minor eye-movements
Like leaf-beings between his fingers:
Remembering the gradual journey
As the softest of sins –

A youthful ribbon, a ray of ink,
A glance at the outskirts of what nature is not,
The astronomical moment of overlap
At the table's corner

Where the knee-to-knee gripped
Transparent curtains
Still harbour the glow
Of his fingerprints.

Michael Coady

Twelve Warm Coats, 1802

> 'My kind and Constant friend Joe Hearn was buried. He left £500 to the poor and Twelve Warm Riding-coats to 12 men of the town whom his Executors (myself and Richard Sause) would deem most in need.'
> – Ms diary, 1787-1809, of James Ryan, Carrick-on-Suir

Who the chosen twelve were
we will never know

nor whether some sold off the gift
for want of food or drink

or whether all stayed clad
against the cold and rain

until the coats outwore them
to serve others in their turn

down to famished tatters
on fetid straw.

No shred of this remains, with
kind and constant friends

and twelve men warmly
clothed from the grave

and every stitch and seam
of every coat, and all

poor flesh they sheltered
long since dust. All gone,

all gone – but for quill
and candlelight, a warm

hand telling of a kindness
done, reaching

beyond clay to touch
this hand in turn.

Vincent Woods

On being asked to write a poem against the war

All I can think of
  is a woman walking
    in the ruins of Dresden
      with her roasted baby
        in a cardboard suitcase
          tied with rope

And in Baghdad

  after a flood
    eyeballs scalp
      shards of bone
floating up through
      the grille
of an air raid shelter
    ten years
  after the bomb

Bitter Legend

When the Jews were expelled from Spain
  they travelled east.

After many days they stopped to rest;
  a message dropped down
        from the sky

'Po-lin,' it said in Hebrew:
  'Stay here.'

That is how Poland got its name.

Denis Collins

The Peace

I have lived
through the great peace,
saw Kennedy fall,
heard the pain
in Mahalia's sorrow song
for Mister King,
watched that little girl
running towards me
burning herself
into my heart,
heard the cries
from Sharpeville,
saw a young man carry
his brother into history,
gathered the names
round me for comfort
Derry, Dublin, Loughgall,
Abercorn, the Falls,
heard Victor Hara
cry an anguished song
as Pinochet rolled
his tanks into Santiago.

I have seen the peace
in my time,
waited two whole summers
for Reagan
to bomb the world,
heard the skulls clatter
one onto the other,
somewhere far away,
far in the east.

I live with the screams
of women and children
raped for Amin and Islam,
for Israel and Palestine
and always for the USA;
I remember the Belgrano,
Rodney King kicked and beaten,
the Contras, Serbia, Bosnia,
that man kneeling in fear
before his head
ricochetted into death,
felt the machete
sink into Hutu flesh,
into Tutu flesh,
cried at CNN
demanding timetables
for Scuds and tanks.

I have lived through the peace
and I don't feel like singing.

Doug Anderson

Phan Thiet
– for Thuy Le

You speak to me
of walking through the village
with your grandfather,
his slow ramble, your love
of all miracles equally
(the pigs the sugar cane the hanging ducks)
when suddenly he gathers you up
like a bundle of long-stemmed flowers
and runs. Sputter of
automatic weapons behind you.
A scream. Before that,
inside your mother,
the shared blood pumping faster,
swelling your little heart.
Soldiers in the village
probing thatch with bayonets.
The kicked-over rice.
The family altar
scattered in the dirt.
And now when you take
the steaming tea
in both hands, for me
you are lifting the red cloth
from the mirrors,
letting the memory
pour into the room.
You look into the green well
of the teacup,
the warmth passing
through your fingers into your eyes.

Doug Anderson

The Torturer's Apprentice

Almost a man now,
he used to shudder
when the old man
slipped hatpin under fingernail
but now he's got
the master's calm,
the seducer's whiskey drift
to ply his subject
to give up his neighbour, tease
from him how many,
where and when.
Next month he'll have his first,
no more dabbing the old man's brow
with a cool towel,
no more sopping up the blood,
spraying air-freshener
to mask the lingering stink
of fear and anguish.
They've saved a little nun
for him, some dear thing
who still believes
that deep down people
are good.
We don't have to do this, Sister,
he'll say,
like a doctor, like a priest,
like he who giveth more
than you ever wanted.
Tell me
what I want to know
and I'll send you to God
with a single bullet in the nape.
You do not want
to finish this poem.
You do not want
to know who writes the check.
You do not want to know the fugitive self
you've sent down there,
where people do those things.
Where people do those things.

Jo Slade

Pegasus Bridge, Benoville, France: 09/07/99.
– for S. W.

My father crossed this bridge on the way to Ranville
on D-Day.
"What's amazing is..."

    To say the least. What was it ?
I mean, what it meant in the End

                                          Is

    We Are Free
    (in so far as we can be.)
What's amazing is...the way Stars reappear.
The same hemisphere.The same North declination.

Myth says, *"His hoof hit the ground
        and a fountain sprung forth."*

So much Blood resurgent.

Freedom means: Not being a Slave. A Prisoner.
Freedom to create.
*"What's amazing is, the sound of traffic crossing.
A constant Clip Clump."*

Hart called it, *The Full Ebb. The Spread. The Turn.*
What he meant was: The sun fell on a town.
                Everything burnt -
                80,000 burnt into the ground.

In the End. Immolation.
You.   *You who are passing...*

Huu Thinh

Asking

I ask the earth: How does earth live with earth?
– We honour each other.

I ask water: How does water live with water?
– We fill each other up.

I ask the grass: How does grass live with grass?
– We weave into one another
  creating horizons.

I ask man: How does man live with man?

I ask man: How does man live with man?

I ask man: How does man live with man?

*– Translated from the Vietnamese by
George Evans and Nguyen Qui Duc*

George Evans

Addendum
Constitution
Erratum

Fell
ow
citizens
of the universe and the rest, this
to inform you you have
30 seconds
to
abandon
all ideas
of having
thirty more
to think about
what to do, that
is: we never take
yes for an answer so
when you reach the
end of this your
30 seconds are
through

Ann Killough

Anniversary (September 11, 2002)

It was what always happens, it had never happened before.
It could not have been expected, of course we should have expected it.
It was because we were too naive, it was because we were guilty.

It was because we were only human.

It was on account of the angel of death,
it was on account of the angel of the hunger for death.
It was on account of the angel of certain retaliation,
it was on account of the angel of reality.

It was on account of the angel of reality.

It was accompanied by stories, there was a progression.
A progression opened itself up, a scaffolding, there was an infolding
                                                      of stories.
Stories settled against the wings of the angels, who remained.

(All of it was what always happens, we should have known).
(All of it was what always happens, we should have done something else).
(All of it was nothing new, there was nothing to be ashamed of).

Stories rose up in the rest of the world like an army of angels.
Stories gathered in the rest of the world, we did not understand.
We did not understand, we gathered the stories against us.
We gathered ourselves against the stories, we went to war.

It was on account of the angel of death,
it was on account of the angel of the hunger for death.
It was on account of the angel of certain retaliation,
it was on account of the angel of reality.

It was on account of the angel of reality.

Daisy Zamora

When I See Them Passing By

When I see them passing by I ask myself sometimes: What must
they feel, the ones who decided to be perfect and keep their marriages
afloat against all odds no matter how their husbands turned out
(party animal womaniser gambler troublemaker
loud-mouthed violent headbanger lunatic weirdo slightly abnormal
neurotic obsessive clearly unbearable
dumbbell deadly boring brute insensitive grubby
egomaniacal ambitious disloyal politicker crook traitor liar
rapist of daughters torturer of sons emperor of the house
tyrant everywhere) but they put up with it
and God only knows what they suffered.

When I see them passing by so dignified and aged
their sons and daughters gone from the house leaving them alone
with a man they once loved (perhaps he's calmed down
doesn't drink hardly talks spends his time with TV
walks in slippers yawns falls asleep snores wakes up early
is ailing harmless almost childish) I ask myself:

Do they dare imagine themselves widows dreaming some night they
                                                        are free
and coming at last without guilt back to life?

                      – translated by George Evans and Daisy Zamora

Deirdre Brennan

Ar iarraidh

Foras ná faoiseamh ní bheidh agam
go dtiocfad lá éigin ar a chorp,
pé fuílleach nó cnáfairt dem mhac a bheidh ann
théis feannadh na doininne is éin chreiche na mara

Is suarach an sólás dom fánaireacht chainte
iad siúd a mhaíonn go bhfuil sé beo;
a deireann go bhfillfidh sé chugam;
nach bhfuil ann ach gur scoitheadh a óige de

Maith is cuimhin liom mar a d'airigh mé
mí-shuaimhneas do-inste an anbháis
amhail néal dorcha ar foluain os cionn
na feorann mar a thánathas ar a charr

Ag siúl na duimhche dom na laethe seo
cuardaím an mhuiríneach dó ina dtom 's ina dtom;
ní fhágaim turscar ná feamainn trá gan iompú,
poll ná pollán sna carraigeacha gan féachaint ann

Mise, nach bhfuil in ann siolla dem shúil
a thabhairt ar an éan róin marbh i mbéal an uisce
a chasann ó ghogaire ina leircín sa ghaineamh,
cad a dhéanfad le broicleach linbh mo bhroinne féin?

Ach fós, is tromluí gach lá nach dtagaim air
's mé ar mearbhall lena ghuth ag glaoch orm
ó phrócóg nach dtig liom a fháil,
na macallaí dom thimpeallú go n-aimsíonn
n-uaigh laistigh díom féin

Bei Dao

Ramallah

in Ramallah
the ancients play chess in the starry sky
the endgame flickers
a bird locked in a clock
jumps out to tell the time

in Ramallah
the sun climbs over the wall like an old man
and goes through the flea market
looking brightly into
a rusted copper plate

in Ramallah
gods drink water from an earthen jar
a bow asks a string for directions
a boy sets out to inherit the ocean
from the edge of the sky

in Ramallah
its seeds sowed along the high noon
death blossoms outside my window
resisting, the tree gets a hurricane's
violent original shape

– translated by Eliot Weinberger

Anna Woodford

Guernica

We wandered around the Spanish gallery
which had been converted from a hospital
after the war. Pictures occupied the space
left by bodies. We weren't getting on,
Nothing was new under the sun.
I didn't see the horse coming.
It charged down the wall into my head,
battling with the spear in its side,
the stones of paint hurled at its body.

Back on home territory,
I cut the picture to size and
propped it above our dwindling fire
(the landlord didn't allow us to
hang up anything permanently).
On the night you left,
the horse's wound looked raw,
I reached out to touch it as though the paint
would come away wet under my fingers.

John E Smelcer

This Is Just To Say
after a poem by William Carlos Williams

a note tacked to a tree in Indian country

we have
torn up the treaties
you signed
only yesterday

which you
paid for
in blood

We're sorry
but we need
your land
so green, so green

# § German Poetry in Translation §

Paul Celan was born in 1920 in Czernowitz into a German-Jewish family. During the war he lost his parents in concentration camps, and was himself interned in a forced labour camp. From 1948 on he lived in Paris, where he ended his own life in 1975. He is considered the major poet in the German language since the war.

Anabasis

This
strait (between walls) written
impassably-true
Upwards and Backwards
into the heart-bright future.

There.

Syllable –
jetty, sea-
coloured, far out
into pathlessness.

Then:
buoy-,
sorrowbuoy-lane
with those
leaping breath-reflexes,
beautiful seconds -: light-
bells' chiming (*dum -,
dun -, un -,
unde -, suspirat
cor*),
re-
leased, re-
deemed, ours.

Visibles, audibles, the
tent-word becoming ever more free:

Twogether.
        – translated by Peter Jankowski and Brian Lynch

Paul Celan

Glimmer-Tree

A word
to which I did not mind losing you:
the word
Never.

It was, and at times you knew it too,
it was
a freedom.
We swam.

Do you still know that I sang?
With the glimmer-tree I sang, the helm.
We swam.

Do you still know that you swam?
Open you lay before me,
you lay for me, you lay
for me before
my for-
ward leaping soul.
I swam for us both. I swam not.
The glimmer-tree swam.

Swim did it? It was
but a puddle all round. It was the infinite pool.
Black and infinite, so it hung,
so it hung world-downwards.

Do you still know that I sang?

This –
o this drift.

Never. World-downwards. I sang not. Open
you lay before
my wayfaring soul.

– translated by Peter Jankowski and Brian Lynch

Ilse Aichinger was born in 1921. As daughter of a Jewish father her life was in grave danger after the annexation of Austria. She left Vienna after 1945 and settled in London for many years. Now living again in Vienna, she is one of the most innovative and distinguished writers of the post war years.

City Centre

Something comes to mind. Does not rush or turn corners like the carriages wanting to go from Stephansplatz into a side street, but turns the corner like the street itself, contains button shops and coffee houses, opens and conceals much, shows the shop windows and everything on display in front, and leaves the store rooms in the dark.

I know about the chocolate cakes, about the wedding of Joachim and Anna, which they have forgotten, about Jews' Lane where the wind blows. So heaven helps us.

Don't mind the sun becoming dimmer! There are wool and shoes for sale in the side lanes. And a narrow flight of steps, overgrown with grass, leading down.

The places we saw now see us.

Jews' Lane

Cobble stones. No longer do the skulls of sacrificial animals adorn our streets. Our pride has vanished.

Behind our hallways the clocks tick into the grey light. Young men smile and ask for our wishes. No Red Sea roars there. Only our laundry still dries in the east wind. It happened because we didn't wait until nightfall. When the sun set, we started out after it.

And here is the place where we grew tired, here we built houses. Here the sun went down, here we bent our backs without bowing.

Since then grass grows between the cobbles.

Brigitte Oleschinski was born in 1955 in Cologne and lives in Berlin. She has published several collections of poetry; her most recent is *Your Passport is Not Guilty*. (1997)

Seaweed Frozen

onto the strand, and along the top the dusky
    herringbonepromenade the stiff
stolid lamp-ladles, the rubber boots
    marching ahead, for hours and

hours, how they suddenly stick out of the slope, rusty ankles
in the uncovered border barrier. The right foot Polish, the
    sell-by date
missing. The left

a hook, that was my child. He fled
in a zigzag, flowed

through the wire; I saw ten toes
walking

on the water

Johannes Bobrowski was born in 1917 in Tilsit, and died in East Berlin in 1965. The plains and great rivers of Pomerania and East Prussia are Bobrowski's poetic homeland. A large part of his work mourns the lost peoples of those regions, the Jews and gypsies among them.

Memorial Leaf

Years,
spiders' threads,
the great spiders, years –
the gypsies with horses
came travelling
the mud path. The old zingaro
came with his whip, the women
stood in the yard gate, talking
arms folded,
cradling the handful of luck.

Later they were seen no more.
Then the stranglers came with leaden
eyes. Once the old woman
up under the roof
asked for the disappeared.

Hear the rain stream
down the slope, they walk,
whom no one sees anymore,
on the old mud path,
shrouded in the fine spray
of water, wind-crowns of strange lands
above their black hair,
lightly.

Johannes Bobrowski

Elderflower

Here comes
Babel, Isaac.
He says:
During the pogrom
when I was a child,
my pigeon,
they tore
its head off.

Houses in wooden streets
elder trees over fences.
The threshold
scrubbed white
down the small steps –
That time, you know,
the trickle of blood.

People, you talk: Forget –
The young are coming
their laughter like bushes of elder.
People, the elder may
die
from your forgetting.

Ingeborg Bachmann was born in 1926 in Klagenfurt, Austria, and died in Rome in 1973. Her first collection, *Die gestundete Zeit* (1953), was an immediate success, and her poetry, narrative prose and essays are revered for their daring, clarity of thought and passion.

No Delicacies

Nothing pleases me anymore

Am I to doll up a metaphor
with an almond blossom?
crucify the syntax
on a dazzling effect?
Who'd want to wrack their brains
over such superfluous things?

I've learned understanding
for the words
which are
(for the lowest class)

hunger
       shame
              tears
and
                     darkness

I will make do
with the uncleansed sob,
with despair
(and I'll despair from despair)
about all the misery,
the general ill-health, the cost of living.

I don't neglect my writing
but myself.
The others know
god knows
how to help themselves with words.
I'm not my assistant.

Am I to
take a thought captive
lock it into the brightly lit cell of a sentence?
Pamper eye and ear
with delicious morsels of words?
explore the libido of a vowel,
establish the collector's value of our consonants?

Must I
with this scatterbrain
and a cramp in this writing hand
under three hundred night long pressure
tear up the paper
sweep away the word operas I plotted
thus destroying: I you and he she it

we you?

(Let it. Let the others.)

My part, let it go lost.

Ingeborg Bachmann

Bohemia Lies On The Sea

If houses here are green, I'll venture in a house.
If bridges here are strong, I'm walking on firm ground.
If love's labour is lost, I'll gladly lose it here.

If it's not me, it's one, who is as good as me.

If a word still borders on me here, I'll let it border.
If Bohemia's still on the sea, I'll trust the seas again.
And if I trust the sea still, then I hope for land.

If it's me, then it is everyone, who is as much as me.
I want no more for myself. I want to run aground.

Aground – that means ashore, I'll find Bohemia
    there.
Shipwrecked and grounded, I wake up at rest.
I know about the deep now and I am unlost.

Come here, Bohemians all, seafarers, whores and
    ships
without their moorings. Would you not be Bohemian, you Illyrians,
    Veronese
Venetians all. Enact the comedies that make us laugh
    enough

To make us cry. And err a hundred times
just as I erred and never passed the tests,
and yet I did pass them, time after time.

Just as Bohemia having passed them one fine day
was pardoned to the sea and since lies on the water.

I border on a word still and another land,
I border, little though it is, on all things more and more,

a Bohemian, a vagrant, who owns nothing, whom nothing holds,
with just the gift to glimpse my chosen land
    from the contested sea.

Erich Fried was born to Austrian-Jewish parents in 1921 in Vienna. After his father was murdered by the Gestapo, Fried fled to London, where he worked for the BBC for many years. Fried's critical political opinions are given free expression in his poems, and he managed in an unique way to combine lyrical subtlety with acerbic satirical wit. He died in 1988 in London.

Questions About Poetry After Auschwitz

Whether it rose as a small brown bird
from the smoke of the crematoria
and stopped for a rest on one of the birches
of Birkenau

whether it flew closer
drawn by the girls' screams
and watched the rapes
and then

sang its song of quiet love
to the dust of ruined cities
and the ballad of ripening corn
to the starving

Whether it grew up in the shadow of money
and lent it its voice
because the coins had grown too big
to still be able to jingle

Whether it flew through the world
and learnt its appreciation of beauty
from the multiple colours
of torn bodies

from the bright blaze of village huts
or the reflections
of the changing daylight
in glazed-over eyes

Whether it built its nest in the end
in a chemically defoliated tree
from hair   shreds of paper   rags
and bloody feathers it had salvaged

and is now waiting for its mate
for the sitting on its eggs
and the hatching of its always
and again innocent young

is known only to lyrical poets
who are constantly appealing
for the protection of birds in a world
soon to be perfect again

Journalists' Club

Look out for friends
who share
your opinion
it's worth it

even if you find
that they're not quite
of the same opinion as you
and that it's worth it

to sacrifice
a little
of your opinion
for harmony's sake

Friendship
becomes firm and reliable
through such
compromises

being opinionated
is less efficient
and useful
than consensus

Did you ever
have
an opinion?
You've got influence now

Hans Magnus Enzensberger was born in Kaufbeuren in 1929, and lives in Munich. He is regarded as the most provocative, outstanding and influential poet, essayist, editor, translator, and analyst of contemporary affairs in Germany today.

The Great Goddess

She mends and mends
bent over her broken darning egg,
a piece of thread between her lips.
Day and night she mends.
Constantly new runs, new holes.

Sometimes she nods off,
for just one moment,
a century long.
With a jolt she wakes up
and mends and mends.

How tiny she has become,
tiny, blind and wrinkled!
With her thimble she gropes
for the holes in the world
and mends and mends.

Hans Magnus Enzensberger

Equisetum

The thing about the horsetail is this:
it, too, was a lot bigger that time,
a few hundred million years ago.
Devonian, Permian, Keuper –
those were the days.

Later on its delicate shoots
served grandmother
to clean dirty pots with.
Now it's not used anymore,
though we scrape
from the deep and burn
its ancestors still.

The horsetail ignores us,
doesn't need us, multiplies discreetly.
It bides its time in the muddy ditch,
simpler than we are
and therefore invincible.
Calmly the gigantic future
awaits its splendid geometry.

Hans Magnus Enzensberger

The Declaration of War Explained

In the backroom of the beer hall,
where seven drunks have gathered together;
war begins; it smoulders
in the kindergarten; the Academy
of Science hatches it out;
no, it thrives in the maternity ward
of Gori or Braunau, on the Internet,
in the mosque; the small brain
of the patriotic poet secretes it;
because someone felt insulted, because someone
licked blood, in God's name
war rages, because of skin colour,
in the bunker, in jest, or by mistake;
because sacrifices have to be made
for the salvation of mankind, especially
at night, due to the oil fields;
also, because even self-mutilation
has its attractions, and because money flows,
war begins, in a delirium,
because of the lost football match;
far from it, for heaven's sake; well, then;
although no one wanted it; I see;
just like that, for fun, heroically,
and because we can't think
of anything better to do.

W.G. Sebald was born in Wertach in 1944. He taught at the University of East Anglia in Norwich for many years, and published, to great acclaim, numerous literary essays as well as prose works such as *The Emigrants* and *Austerlitz*. The excerpt here is taken from *Elementargedicht Nach der Natur* (1988). Sebald died in a car accident in England in 2001.

from **Elementargedicht Nach der Natur**

IV

Lord, I dreamt that in order
to see the Battle of Alexander
I had flown specially to Munich.
It was just getting dark
and far below me I saw
the roof of my house, saw shadows
stretching across the eastern
English countryside, I saw
the hem of the island, the waves
rolling up on the sand
and the ships on the North Sea immobile
in front of their foam-white tracks.
Like a ray hovering in the depths
of the sea I glided along without
making a sound hardly moving
a wing high above the earth,
above the mouth of the Rhine
and followed upstream
the road of water now
turned heavy and bitter.
The cities phosphorescent on the banks,
the smouldering industrial plants
waiting below plumes of smoke
like ocean liners for the sound
of the horn, the flickering lights
of rail- and motorways, the murmuring
of mussels of woodlice and leeches
multiplying a millionfold, the icy decay,
the groaning within ribs of rock,
the mercury glint, the clouds

rushing through the towers of Frankfurt,
the extended and the accelerated time,
all this passed through my senses
and was already so near the end
that each breath caused the vision
to shudder. Mountain oaks on the slopes
of the Odenwald heaved like the tide
then a desert followed and wasteland
where the wind drove
the stone dust through valleys.
A twice sharpened sword separated
the earth and the sky, a radiance
flowed into space and the final
destination of my outing, the vision
of Altdorfer opened up before me.
More than a hundred thousand,
proclaim the inscriptions
numbered the dead, over whom
the battle surges for the salvation
of the occident in the rays
of a sinking sun.
Just now the battle's fortunes are turning.
In the centre of the grandiose melée
of banners and flags, lances and
spears and shafts, the bodies
of men and beasts in armour,
Alexander on his white steed, the Western world's
hero and before him fleeing
towards the moon's crescent
Darius, the look of sheer terror
on his face. The crafty priest
who had hung up an oil print
of the battle painting next to the blackboard
described the outcome of things
as fortuitous. It was, he said, proof
of the necessity of the destruction
of all the hordes emerging from the East

and thus part of the history of salvation.
Since then I read in a different
teacher's book that death
hangs before us perhaps like
the painting of the battle of Alexander
on the walls of the school room.
I now know, that like with the eye
of a crane you survey
its vast territory, truly
an Asiatic spectacle,
and that slowly you learn from the minuscule
figures and the incomprehensible
beauty of nature arching above them,
to see that side of life
you had not seen before. We gaze
at the battle scene and
looking from North to the South
we glimpse a camp of white
Persian tents lying in evening light
and a city on the coast.
Out on the ocean ships travel
with bellying sails and the shadows
already touch Cyprus and beyond
stretches the mainland of Egypt.
One can make out the delta of the Nile,
the Sinai Peninsula, the Red Sea and
further away in the distance
in dwindling light the towering
snow-and-ice mountain ranges
of the strange, unexplored and
African continent.

Silke Scheuermann was born in Karlsruhe in 1973 and lives in Frankfurt Am Main. In Spring 2001, she received the Leonce und Lena Prize for her first collection *Der Tag ad dem die Möwen zweistimmig sangen*, from which this poem is taken. Her work has been praised for its individual style and ironic melancholy.

Requiem for
a Recently-Conquered Planet
with Intensive Radiation

But what will happen once we've told each other all our stories
ten thousand hot stories

when the encyclopedia of our pipe-dreams has been spelled from A to Z
and we've worn out our star like the sofa

on which we came to know each other very well
when we then sit silently by the window and smoke

Nights of almost perfect stillness
in which only your last sentences resonate

They were talking about the two of us
that in fact we're celestial bodies

possessing such strong gravitational force
they don't even let go of their own light

therefore don't shine but are black
tellers of tales burnt by their tongues

Sarah Kirsch, born in 1935 in Limlingerode, now lives in Northern Germany. She has published many collections of poetry and several prose works. Her distinctive tone, combines natural colloquial speech with highly lyrical and formal elements, has won her many prizes for her poetry.

Vanishing Point

Heine walked through the mountains
He dawdled in houses, on squares
And took two weeks for the distance
We'd have travelled in one day
Our journeys take us from one country
Straight into the next mere details
Can't be allowed to detain us
Our own machines force us
To race on without tarrying expeditions
Into the souls of people have been denied us
The rubble tips labyrinths beautiful realms
Remain unexplored and hidden
The waiters don't need our tidings
They get their news from television
There are different cars one type of human
Everything is exchangeable wherever we are

Sarah Kirsch

The Plain

>...my beloved
>vales smile at me.

The great images daily
Pure clarity of the air sharp
Lines around grasses and clouds at night
The plate of the moon on the water
The flying creatures of the earth
Large rising bodies their gentle
Necks offered up trustingly
To the wind how could I
Get tired of naming it
Bitterness sinks far and wide the sorrow
Into our joyfulness swept away
Like the leaves of the tree the
Dancing autumnal midges
After a strong frost though we are
Destroyed even before our breath fails us
How serene would be our leave-taking
If with the lighthearted certainty
That this earth will last
For a long time yet
We could gladly depart

Michael Krüger was born in 1943 and lives in Munich, where he is the editor of the prestigious publishing house Hanser Verlag. He has published many collections of poetry, among them *Diderot's Katze*, *Wettervorhersage* and *Archive des Zweifels*.

Night Flight

Because all airplanes landed too late
and weren't allowed to lift off anymore,
we, the stragglers, a polyglot group,
were put on a plane which was already out of service.

I sat on seat 34-B in the unpopular middle,
to my right a black-as-night angel,
sorting out his rubbish, cool as you please,
to my left a gent reading Plato in the original.

It wasn't forbidden to smoke, in row 20
a hookah was even employed.
Football was played in the aisle and in the front
in business class an Irish band practiced

the requiem by Verdi. I, too, imagined
my old age would be different,
said the tired stewardess passing round copies
of last year's newspapers. The pilot smiled

in his sleep. Nobody gets to where he wants to go,
growled the angel, and Plato nodded off.
Towards morning when my eyes closed
we went up in the air.

Michael Krüger

At First Glance

Nothing really seems to have changed:
The chestnut in front of the house, tortured by ivy,
the plum trees on their blue carpet,
the sweet smell of childhood and decay.
The thunder of lorries from the valley
and the shadow running quickly around the house
against the hands of the clock, probing grief.
Even the fountain stills stands like a poem.
When I looked in, a face creased by frogs
greeted me from below, from the bottom.
His mouth was wide open as if he wanted to scream.
Only the roads round the village have multiplied
and one of them leads straight through my heart.
But otherwise nothing has changed.

Durs Grünbein was born in Dresden in 1962 and lives in Berlin. He has published several collections of poetry and is considered the great poetic talent of the younger generation, due to his iconoclasm and mastery of traditional lyrical forms.

Monologic Poem No. 2

Now and then there are
in-between days when

I feel again like starting
a poem of the type

which is still not
very popular. I mean

one without meta-
physical finesse or

what these days is deemed
its *ersatz*... this cynical ploy

of sinking down on your knees before
history marching forward on stilts,

or as you breathe your last in the
tough East-West marathon,
of moaning about a pain in your side

like the best of Dante's
damned shadows. Poems

somebody recently told me
captivated him only if they
were full of surprises

written down in those
strange moments when

something still vague
a daydream a single

line begins anew and

seduces.

Durs Grünbein

September Elegies
for Jane Kramer

I

Then the excitement dies down. From the sight of the supernova
Most people recover at work, game of fortune and sex.
What remains of mementos in the end is a quiet "It's over."
You pray in silence, fold your paper, drink your Becks,
Return to the Lilliput-tightness of the quotidian, mull,
If you escaped, over your neighbour's fate, who was struck by
                                                                                                the hammer
Destiny, made by sleepers now seems remote-controlled:
That airplanes are bombs hardly disturbs the technical
                                                                                                slumber.
Ashamed you sometimes look at the sky. What flies there
Could be an archangel on his way to a fire signal as usual.
The steam from hot food stalls in the streets smells of fresh war.
Compared to the drama of the cockroach life is pretty banal.
No one's a stoic here. Outside thresholds and doorways you parley,
Driven by appointments and debts you rush through the city.
No one's had time to extract anything like mental peace
From the certainty of death and that everything will end?
Next day the child grins again with a knocked-out tooth,
The globe makes its rounds just as before. From above it all
The spot in Manhattan looks like an inactive volcano.
Skyscrapers too – their construction lasts years, seconds their fall.

Peter Waterhouse was born in 1956 in Berlin, and lives in Vienna. He is a distinguished translator of Ginsberg and Hopkins among others. He is the author of prose pieces, plays and poetry collections, most recently his collection *Blumen*.

Into The Great Entanglement Outside Vienna

Here things begin to talk to each other
a canister says canister
street lamp shines on garden and vegetables
is suddenly a vegetable lamp
motorways lead across carpets and doormats
cars drive into waiting rooms and kitchens
children and schools stand on parking lots
the schools ring, jangle, slam, shrill
jangle, ring, ring, slam

I am at home here, I have nothing here
I have a few bricks in the grass
a few open doors
a whole lot of neon
here are hardly any zebra crossings
here swerves the moon on high
here I have a twisted bicycle
here I have tiny and enormous CD-shops
here many sit and smoke in the dark
and the people visiting the ballroom cross the parking lot

the little mountains over there are no different from my teeth
the canister is no different from my thought
the tree is no different from my children
the automobile is no different from my shoes.
The kings on the bikes aren't totally different from me
and the station loudspeaker calls: all tickets
from the Basque country to the southern
outskirts of Athens

A stone can be a flower
and one or the other in the village
would like to taste the ashes of the dead

There's as much love here as supermarket assistants
there's as much love here as the flamboyant hairstyles
or straight hair
the narrow death cars drive into the life bureaus
and the Mafia jeeps drive to Vienna and Moscow

Trousers, shoes, hats, heirlooms,
excretions, skid marks, love,
hairstyles, tennis courts: Not the sun
but the tennis ball shines at 6.46
I can recognize friendships and tennis balls

Thomas Böhme was born in Leipzig in 1955, where he still lives. A writer of prose and poetry, his verse collection *Die Cola Trinker*, containing work from almost two decades of writing, was published in 2000.

> SO MANY islands it's impossible
>   to visit them all. And on all of these islands
>   the same black pianos you're not
>   permitted to touch.
> Only the harpsichord you constantly hear is made of brown
>   wood.
> It probably follows our ears on a ship adrift and
>   zigzagging across the lagoon for this sole purpose.
> The name of the pianist remains unspoken. But you
>   know he's one of the best, and he'd never perform without
>   his spotted Great Dane.
> Perhaps they play four-handed. This might explain the growling
>   in the lower registers.
> The graveyard isle possesses a walled-in organ whose
>   sullen bass pipes summon back
>   all of the dead who try to depart
> The sea on the other hand is so shallow here you
>   could walk across it.
> Of course no one comes upon the idea. The music
>   after all is not intended for paddlers.
> Who are the smooth-running boats for,
>   if not for us, the living.
> The music provides them with a mild climate and takes care
>   that the winds permanently blow from the south.
> But sometimes it rains for days. Then the pianos
>   seek refuge below PVC tarpaulins.
> They remind one of sad cows who have stopped singing
>   because they stand alone, each on her own island.
> No matter what they tell us – and the boatswains are unstinting
>   with witty anecdotes – we feel sorry for
>   the wooden-legged instruments, which are never allowed
>   to give proof of their art.
> Gladly we would ask the pianist accompany us
>   to the islands at his leisure. With a few scales
>   he might bring the black shrines back to life.

But we never catch sight of him, and his ship – even if
   it occasionally comes within earshot – has never yet docked
   at one of the landing places.
Therefore despite the well-tempered sounds
   that whizz through the air we are left with the lasting impression
   of a mournful muteness.
So many islands, so many pianos!

Sabine Küchler was born in 1965 in Cologne. She has published several collections of poetry, among them *Ich erklär es mir so* (1990).

SO MUCH had happened
that nothing had happened never mind which film
I rushed into the cinema wanted only to see people
who'd talk to me and didn't want to know anything about me
a few thirty-somethings hinted strangely
at their particular way of aloneness their type
of longing a woman stroked a violin with the greatest
of tenderness while a man declared in a strained voice
that he would like to get married now to the one
who during the whole film had done nothing except cut roses
and lie through her teeth I am
so disappointed that nothing can disappoint me any more
said the man just then the violin started to sob
and names ran across the screen
under the friendly gaze of the gods
directed at an unfriendly landscape
light exploded I had been
entirely alone in the cinema except for a bloated
old woman who probably always sat here
under her seat stacks of bottles crumpled tissues like old
dirty snow from her coat trickled
peanut shells she had commented on every disaster
with "There you are!" thereby persuading misfortune
                                                    to stay
I thought because lately I'd acquired the habit
of thinking in the street people ran
so fast I had the sluggish feeling
of grieving stones we had been together
for three days in my flat so quiet
that time had forgotten us we were saying good bye
for three days and nights like stones
which lie beside each other and some one throws one
across the hedge just for fun so much had happened
that nothing had happened at all and nothing more could happen
at least I thought nothing worse I remembered the last
thing I had seen when I left
was the old woman standing again in front of the box office
demanding a ticket for the next film

David Butler

Precision and Restraint

Theodore Deppe, *Cape Clear: New and Selected Poems*, Salmon Publishing, 2002, €10.
John O'Donnell, *Some Other Country*, Bradshaw Books, 2002, €9.
Gerry Murphy, *Torso of an Ex-Girlfriend*, Dedalus Press, 2002, €8.80.

Thumbing through Theodore Deppe's *Cape Clear: New and Selected Poems* with, I have to say, increasing engagement and admiration, I am reminded of the late Raymond Carver, with whom Deppe shares an interest in Anton Chekhov ('A Pair of Earrings', 'Letter to Suvorin'). This common interest is not without significance. Carver and Deppe are both largely anecdotal poets, at their most powerful when dealing in the Chekhovian trump cards of precision and restraint. If violence and empathy strangely cohabit their work, they do so with an understated ubiquity that is all the more convincing for the absence of obviously emotive language.

Perhaps the most striking poems of the present collection are those which draw upon Deppe's extensive experience as a registered nurse prior to his coming to Ireland in 2000. Again, I am put in mind of those evocative lines penned by another American poet, Robert Lowell, when he urges:

> Pray for the grace of accuracy
> Vermeer gave to the sun's illumination
> stealing like the tide across a map
> to his girl solid with yearning.

This grace of accuracy, so pervasive in, say, Carver's 'A New Path to the Waterfall', is readily apparent in Deppe's output. Particularly striking are a group of poems which deal with the troubled child Marisol, 'who'd first / come to our children's unit / when she was five – something broken / behind those eyes, and fierce... ' ('Marisol'). In an earlier poem ('The Japanese Deer'), we learn that she was 'raped repeatedly by her mother's boyfriend', and yet was able, on a particular outing, to climb with another troubled child Luis 'for a short time / above the brambled understory, outside history, / discovered a fragrant scent on their hands, / shredded more petals, rubbed the smell deep in their skin.'

But arguably the most effective, and disturbing, of the Marisol poems is the astonishing 'The Book of God'. In place of simple outrage or pathos, this poem, together with 'Admission, Children's Unit', provides us a glimpse into the complexity of the abused child's perspective. In the latter, a boy who was held down by his mother while her boyfriend inflicted on him 'six wounds, raised, ashy, second / or third degree, arranged in a cross' nevertheless 'anchored himself to her. Glared at me', so that finally 'It took four of us to pry him from his mother's arms.' In the former poem, the child Marisol pins up as a 'bedside shrine' a photo from *Newsweek* of a crucified Bosnian girl: 'when I took the picture from her wall she dug / her nails in my wrist, tried to bite my hand.' Finally she accepts a notepad upon whose cover she writes 'THE BOOK OF GOD / CAME BACK AS A SMALL GIRL. / On each page she drew pictures she couldn't talk about.' A more manipulative poet might have tried to get more mileage out of the presence of the cross in each anecdote; Deppe is content merely to register the detail, and it remains the more powerful a presence precisely to the extent that it has not been obviously exploited.

For the past few years, Theodore Deppe has been living in the remoter parts of Ireland with his wife Annie, who is a constant presence in the Cape Clear section of the book. Here, too, Deppe is on his guard against the temptation in poetry to mythologize: '"If you see the lark, don't let it become a symbol / in some damn poem of yours. For Christ's sake / let it be itself..."' warns his friend Chuck in the poem 'Recitative on Cape Clear Island'. Indeed, the aforementioned 'The Japanese Deer', taken from the 1996 *The Wanderer King* collection, might be read as a meditation on this very theme – its dedication reads 'For Denny Lynn, who likes to know what's true in my poems and what's "made up".' The balance, one feels, is overwhelmingly on the side of the true. This is writing of the highest order.

If a good number of the poems making up John O'Donnell's inaugural collection, *Some Other Country*, are grounded in autobiographical detail, he shows himself ready on occasion to move imaginatively beyond the world of lived experience. The collection has, as its centre of gravity, a sequence of six sonnets entitled 'New Testimonies'. These review the Passion of Our Lord from six unique perspectives which include, unexpectedly, the Last Supper's landlord, Barabbas, the Cross itself and – perhaps with the Velasquez painting at the National Gallery in mind – a Kitchen Maid at Emmaus. Framing the sequence, unobtrusively, with complementary supper scenes gives a good sense of the care with which O'Donnell habitually approaches his craft, and these two end-pieces are, to my mind, also the most achieved in terms of narrative register. Only occasionally are these poems less than subtle, as when the Cross of sonnet IV 'took flame; became / Smoke billowing from ash. And rose again.'

Immediately following the 'New Testimonies' sequence are several of the collection's most accomplished poems. 'O'Neill in Rome' imagines the great Earl's exile, unnerved by the 'ruthless opulence' of his new milieu. He misses Ulster cattle raids, 'The ditch and thorn in league with us', laments 'the rattle / Of informers' coins', and here one senses a contemporary resonance to the poem. This is emphasised by the sense of sectarian menace that underlies the poem 'Fault', which immediately follows: 'The past is pushing up under our feet // Along this seismic fault we live upon / Where words like 'tribe' and 'territory'/ Cause tremors.' It also sounds a theme of historic and contemporary interest to which O'Donnell will return; that of human migration.

En passant, there are a number of less convincing moments, however. The poem 'Rhino' ambles so inevitably towards the beast's encounter with the high-powered rifle that one balks at investing the subject with the interest it should merit. A sense of the obvious or hackneyed also attends several of the early schoolroom memoirs. Elsewhere, O'Donnell's option to rhyme, itself laudable, can have the effect of introducing something contrived into a poem – the culminating rhyme of 'Kola's Shop' seems rather too pat; conversely, a sense of the unreal is intensified in the various arrested tableaux of 'The Hook' by the use of patently intrusive rhyming (as for instance when 'deli' rhymes with 'TV', and 'back at' with 'jacket'). In general, O'Donnell is on surer ground when he moves out of nostalgia mode, and the title poem is a fine meditation on emigration, perhaps recalling Eavan Boland: 'voices struggling to find / A language adequate to their exile'.

There are echoes of Boland too in the earlier 'Sports Day', with its description of the 'Suburban Pastoral', and of the Ted Hughes of 'Full Moon and Little Frieda' in O'Donnell's 'Watching Stars'. Which is not to say that the poet is suffering unduly from what Harold Bloom diagnosed as the 'anxiety of influence'; only that he must remain careful his chunks of influence don't remain undigested.

Torso of an Ex-Girlfriend, Gerry Murphy's fifth collection, not only suggests no anxiety of influence, it positively flaunts the manifold influences the poet has variously imbibed. A prefatory poem entitled 'As For Dante' sets the agenda, reworking 'Nel mezzo del cammin di nostra vita / mi ritrovai per una selva oscura / ché la diritta via era smarrita' to give 'Halfway along my appointed way, / whistling cheerfully in a vast forest / I strayed hopelessly from the path.' If this were intended as translation it would be cavalier indeed. It is rather, in the tradition of a Lowell, a Carson or a Muldoon, the free appropriation of an idea or conceit, itself as often as not already once removed by intermediary translation from the original. Indeed, the inclusion of Heaney, Levertov and Yeats as springboards for versions emphasises the point that translation is here a conceptual rather than linguistic concern. Four of Murphy's poems have as title 'After Yeats', 'After Sorescu', 'After Yesenin' and 'After Seferis', while no fewer than fifteen employ the same formula as epigraph, acknowledging sources as various as Goethe, Catullus, Cavafy, Arrian and Barthes. One, 'The Poet Tells of his Fame', invokes an entire translational hall of mirrors worthy of Borges himself: (*after Merwin, after Borges, after el Hadrami*).

By ranging over such a wide temporal, spatial and linguistic field, Murphy is perhaps intent on pointing out the extent to which human concerns – in particular those pertaining to the male of a certain age – are universal. If this is the case, then some of the re-workings are considerably successful, though one would like to know the liberality with which Murphy has enlisted the originals. 'Ode 32', after Catullus, seems to me particularly succinct in registering the flippant ennui of a male erotic daydream. By contrast, 'Into the Small Hours' is little more than a dismal list of anatomical detail unable or unwilling to uncouple itself from pornographic adjectival cliché. The same lack of consistency attends, and mars Murphy's use of haiku and related form. Where the 'Ballynoe Haiku' pairing succeeds in registering the poet's varied reaction to the memory of kisses given and received, the later 'Death and Resurrection' seems trivial, not to say puerile: 'Beloved Gráinne / in the depths of your cleavage / receive my spirit.'

If this kind of inconsistency undermines the collection as a whole, a number of the versions included are consummately handled. One would single out 'Ablutions', after Mandelstam, as particularly well achieved, together with the poem entitled 'After Sorescu', for the Romanian poet with whom Murphy shares a lively sense of the ludic. The collection's penultimate poem, 'The Task Laid Aside', which reworks an idea of Denise Levertov, is also compelling, picturing God as an old man living upstairs who 'shuffles about / muttering in Aramaic.' Unfortunately, the effect is instantly deflated by the triviality of the final poem, scarcely of more interest than a toilet graffito.

The title poem of the collection is of special interest, both insofar as I take it to be, for Murphy, a keynote for the present collection, and equally to the extent that it falls short of the sonnet that inspired it. That it should be out-punched by the weighty meditation 'Archaischer Torso Apollos' is scarcely surprising – one would be reluctant to censor Marcel Duchamp's *L.H.O.O.Q.* for failing to 'live up to' the *Mona Lisa* – yet it is difficult to know what precisely to make of Murphy's invocation of Rilke. There seems little of Duchamp's playfulness, while the single image that does not find its roots in the original is mawkish rather than inventive: 'hair, a midnight garden for all the senses'. Is there an irony intended in the replacement of an ancient stone torso by the memory of a girl's body? If not, are we really to compare Murphy's concluding 'you must change your life' to the ineluctable epiphany 'Du mußt dein Leben ändern'? Or is 'undecideability', that lemma of post-modernism, the point?

The unevenness of the present collection is a pity. In enlisting such an eclectic pantheon of authority, and in the irreverence with which translation is employed, the collection might be understood as a palliative to the use of quotation as artefact by, say, Pound or Eliot. One feels instead that, while a number of the entries might sit well in a future *Selected Poems of Gerry Murphy*, the collection as a whole would have benefited considerably from a far more rigorous use of the editorial red pen.

Ciaran O'Driscoll

Memorable Truth-Telling

Michael Hartnett, *A Book of Strays*, Gallery Press, 2002, €10.
Justin Quinn, *Fuselage*, Gallery Press, 2002, €10.
Susan Connolly, *Winterlight* (illustrations by Anne-Marie Moroney), Flax Mill Publications, 2002, €9.

Michael Hartnett's *A Book of Strays* is a gathering of disparate items ranging from contemporary-style verse not included in his *Collected Poems* to 'songs for the people' in various traditional ballad forms. A bag of liquor-ish allsorts, you might say, as the reek and misery and exhilaration of booze permeate this book, as in 'House Devil':

> ...as I beat my dazed retreat
> at the top of Leeson Street
> the moon shone like a Guinness-bottle label.

A very true image, that, to anyone who has looked closely, for whatever reason, at the label on a Guinness bottle. But the same poem in full is sub-Hartnett:

> With the vodka, 80 proof,
> I though I saw a hoof,
> black and hairy underneath the table;
> perhaps I was in the rats
> but said 'I must go feed my cats'
> and staggered out of there while I was able.

While the 'sub-Hartnett' label can be applied to this collection as a whole, there are gems which sparkle throughout these uneven pages, and many of the pieces will be enjoyed by a wider audience than the habitual readers of poetry. 'Maiden Street Ballad' is a tour de force of popular balladeering, obviously intended to be sung to the same air as 'The Limerick Rake'. The metrics of this piece can only be understood as sung, with the accents falling in all kinds of strange places and frequent tailbacks of slack syllables. But it works as a ballad and has a certain old-fashioned power. Totally lacking in 'bourgeois sentimentality', it has an air of jokey cynicism regarding poverty, misfortune and fleshly ills, and although the greed of shopkeepers is memorably condemned, there is a certain element of mockery in the treatment of the early hardships of the author's family and neighbours, particularly in view of the fact that, with the passing of time, they have bettered themselves:

> We have motorcars now and we sometimes play squash
> and, dirty or clean, quite often we wash;
> we have more than one shirt and more than two socks
> and we holiday in the Canaries.

The autobiographical element resolves itself into an Odyssey of pubs and drinking companions, liked and disliked, but Hartnett manages to intersperse these preoccupations with some finely observed evocations of his hometown's past.

This is certainly a heterogeneous collection. Many of the offerings (such as 'On Those who Stole Our Cat, a Curse') belong purely to the domain of comic and curious verse, and there are some lovely satirical squibs, while the influence of Kavanagh is evident in the (literally) haunting ballad 'The Ghost of Billy Mulvihill', and in 'Who Killed Bobby Sands?', which is a pastiche of Kavanagh's 'Who Killed James Joyce?' (in turn a pastiche of 'Who Killed Cock Robin?'). There is a poem ('Aere Perennius') addressed to Kavanagh himself, lamenting the colonization of the poetry realm by academics:

> ...dull strangers with degrees
> who prune, to fit conceptions
> you would never back,
> your statements and your acts...
>
> ...
>
> Let me escape a similar fate.
> I'd rather be forgotten out of hand
> than wronged in bronze:
> let the sad facts stand.

The last four lines here have a spare beauty that cuts to the chase, and are characteristic of the best of Michael Hartnett, who despite all his foibles was possessed of that essential poetic element – memorable truth-telling.

Compared to Hartnett, Justin Quinn is both urban and urbane:

> We eat at Rez's, Covent Garden,
> up-market Italian, but not outré.
> – 'We eat at Rez's...'

A far cry from Newcastle West and Hartnett's 'Maiden Street Ballad', where...

> We had turnips for dinner, we had turnips for tea,
> and half stones of pandy piled up on our plates...

Quinn's book takes us on a circular journey, from personal concerns to impersonal forces and back. I had a problem immediately with this collection's opening lines, from 'Laurel':

> We sit in the apartment, evening light
> still blue and red though it's now getting late.
> Summer weather is suddenly upon us,
> a sort of strange, extraordinary bonus.
> This whole long winter's ice is edged and shoved
> away and off and down some twisting shaft –
> the awful cold, those months and days and hours,
> two heads locked into darkness, mine and yours,
> as we moved round the streets, then travelled home
> to cook and talk, the central heating's hum
> throughout the honeycomb of our new block.

The purely descriptive, non-evocative tone here and throughout the first poem frequently descends into banality, although some good images flash out here and there ('two heads locked into darkness, mine and yours'). The insistent regularity of the metre generates redundancies. Is the 'bonus' strange or extraordinary, or could there be another single word for it? What's the difference here between 'away' and 'off', and why are we told that the 'whole long winter' consists of 'months and days and hours'? Quinn's discursive, metrically even style has a slackness to it, an invitation to wordiness, hendiadys and hendia-that, 'a kind of X' and 'a sort of Y'. An added unease here (for me) is the slipping in and out of pastiche, the 'blazon heat / of necessary conjunction', the use of spellings like 'tenour', and the general academic feel to what is in fact a celebration of love and the arrival of a child. Such life-events are deserving, I feel, of much sharper realization in poetry, and the piece would have benefited from revision.

A praiseworthy element of Quinn's collection (certainly in an Irish context) is how, even in the very beginning, in the domestic situation, the more discordant, global theme is announced:

> In waves and waves the mixed reports come in.
> ...swirls and gleams
> of rapid imagery and breaking news,
> a pageantry, a kind of global nous.

The book progresses, gradually situating the domestic in the global and globalizing ethos of our times. An image which struck me was that of the family asleep, in 'Our Heads Drop Down':

> trireme
> with all its oars at rest, the gentle wash
> of waves on the hull...

...but the sense of vulnerability was somewhat annulled by my recalling that a trireme was in fact an Ancient Greek warship. There follow a number of poems dealing with the 'fuselage' of the title, the whole framework of a world coming increasingly under electronic surveillance and control, and meshing into a monstrous organism constantly active just below the surface of ordinary life, determining individual destinies. Here the personal voice cedes to the impersonal, and the regularity of the metre falls away into a free verse larded at times with intertextual references and somewhat reminiscent of Pound's *Cantos* or the later Kinsella. These poems have a satiric and angry edge to them which I liked.

'Personal history irrelevant' deals with a contract killing, but its ending pinpoints the general dilemma that Quinn is wrestling with in this part of the book:

> Which the state calls murder, the sudden collapse
> Of a whole world put together by eyes and ears and hands,
>
> a huge horizon cancelled –
> forty banknotes (light, manoeuvrable) changing hands;
>
> subtract one huge horizon
> and still the real one stays there more or less intact.

The fate of the individual in this electronically-meshed world driven by impersonal forces is cleverly dealt with in 'Go through and down the steps', where the poet is attracted to a waitress, and discovers a few days after their 'brief transaction', on finding the receipt in his pocket, that her name is SARKA 03.

Quinn is to be commended for his ambition in this collection. And I mean ambition in a good sense: it is difficult to reconcile irreconcilables. We have the traditional strains of love poetry, lyricism, the joy of life and the awareness of mortality, which are meshed in this poet's broad sensibility with the imponderables of a 'new world order', the creation of some kind of enormous organism which threatens the very fibre of personal significance. A collection of mixed success ends affirmatively, the final poem being a welcome into life of the poet's child. For some reason I am reminded of Michael Hartnett's lines:

> Poets with progress make no peace or pact.
> The act of poetry is a rebel act.

From the global back to the local with Susan Connolly's *Winterlight*, which is an interim chapbook between two collections. There is a lingering sense of some deep personal hurt in these poems, and an affirmation of the healing power of poetry, music and landscape. There is a revitalizing of place through the evocation of the legends attaching to wells and other landmarks, and to animals. Connolly has a natural sense of lyricism which is often very effective, though occasionally she says more than is necessary, determined to fill out the number of lines in her schematic stanzas, or slips into banal statement. She has written a chillingly simple poem about Bettina Poeschel ('In Memory of Bettina Poeschel'), abducted while walking from Drogheda to the Brú na Bóinne Visitors Centre on 23 September 2001:

> But fate struck fast as lightning
> one bright September morning
>
> before we knew your name
> or what you looked like
>
> or how you would be found,
> your glasses smashed beside you.

Another poem that cuts to the lyrical quick is 'One thousand autumn oak leaves.' Its weaving of past, present and future into one coherent fabric has an incantatory power to enchant both writer and reader into an acceptance of life and all that happens. Connolly's poetry seems to have a facility for drawing on mythic energies.

Clíodhna Carney

Poets and Makers

Mary Montague, *Black Wolf on a White Plain*, Summer Palace Press, 2001, €11.50.
Vona Groarke, *Flight*, Gallery Press, 2002, €10.00.
Dennis O'Driscoll, *Exemplary Damages*, Anvil Press, 2002, £7.95.

Should a poet declare (or even have) a poetic credo? Some of the most famous Irish poems of the last thirty years have offered, however subtly, a modus operandi, or an aesthetic that holds true not just for that particular poem, but for that poet's oeuvre as a whole. Seamus Heaney's 'Digging' is an example. These poems are destined to become canonical, to be read again and again and to be set on exam papers for schoolchildren to tease out. Perhaps part of their charm is that they seem to offer the reader a tangible connection to another consciousness, that of the poet.

But if schoolchildren are encouraged to identify the poet in the poem, the more sophisticated reader is warned against it, and is armed instead with the critical tools of voice, speaker, persona, none of which is to be confused with the unreachable poet beyond. Maybe the problem lies with the word 'poet', which we use to mean both the creative artist, and the man or woman at the breakfast table. To ease the confusion in our own era between the person Seamus Heaney and the poet Seamus Heaney, one might think about reviving the medieval category of the 'maker'. Even though our term 'poet' traces its own ancestry back to the Greek word for 'maker', we have largely dumped the distinction implied by both words between the man and the artist. Ours is a fiercely autobiographical era, and we continually refuse or fail to differentiate between the person one is and the artist one becomes in the act of making art. But, for the moment, we can't escape the word 'poet', with all its ambiguity.

Mary Montague's 'My First Experience of Beauty' reads as a guide to the poet's aesthetic, or a declaration of a poetic credo, and invites an identification of the speaker with the poet. Because the experience in question entailed the appearance of horses on the cliffs by Rossnowlagh strand, and because the collection as a whole deals preeminently with finely detailed observations of animals, it is very tempting, if presumptuous, to read the poem in autobiographical ways. 'Meanderings' tends to reinforce the autobiographical impression, as the speaker describes herself as significantly different to her adult peers and relatives, as someone who prefers the childlike state of wonder: 'My cousins have long left the liminal / state I hold to... I no longer / pause on every threshold but some reticence / has stayed through wastrel years, has stood me / at the edge so long it seems to be / the only place I fit in.' The final poem in this debut collection, '26 August 1979', embeds a teenage journal entry in the mature speaker's recollection of her coming-of-age as a poet: 'I close the diary. / I feel as rich as the memory. / It is twenty-one years ago. / The dog, the fox are long / dead; but I am back, back / for the fox, back for the girl, / back for the poet.' The sensitivity of this poet is evident not only in the nature poems, but also in the more questioning, introspective poems such as 'Betrayal', and in the very successful and affecting poems which deal with human subjects, such as 'Intrusion'.

Vona Groarke, in stark comparison, does not offer a credo, but a method. Her opening poem, "The Verb 'to herringbone'", with its tricky, philological title, hints at the intricacy and minuteness of stitch and pattern that characterise the subtle, intelligent poems that follow. Metaphors of sewing have appeared in Vona Groarke's previous two collections. Here the etymology of the verb 'to herringbone' suggests not only the work that must be put in to create the doubling back, 'veering off' pattern, but also the work involved in the unpicking of the stitches, or, to push it too far (although some parallel metaphors of quill, bone, strands, threads and calligraphy maybe excuse this) the deboning of the fish. And certainly, the poems in this collection demand careful readings and re-readings. I still have a few bones in my craw.

Apart from the method, this opening poem also has something important to say about the subjects of the other poems in this collection. Rather than concerning themselves with the concrete, the historical or the autobiographical (although there are important exceptions), these poems, both in methodological and thematic senses, are interested not in what has happened as such, but rather in what might happen or might have happened, or in the things that happen on the underside, in the corners, 'on the lee side of an air'. They are poems 'of the air displaced by flight'. They entail a certain sacrifice – of grandiosity, of grand themes, of flight – and they put themselves forward inauspiciously, tentatively. But the poems assembled on the pages of this collection are in themselves anything but weak. Impeccable formal skills, impressive and sustained control of images, linguistic play and verse forms are all features here of a paradoxical poetry that is both quiet and diminutive but powerful and intense.

These poems are as hypothetical as dreams. Vona Groarke likes to throw down possibilities: 'Say one feather...'; 'Choose one version...' She pursues the permutations of the hypothetical brilliantly in poems like 'The End of the Line', where the speaker considers that coincidences at the level of a shared name might allow one to discover that one has written books entitled *The History of Syphilis* or *Paraguayan Folk Dance*. Historical fact is abandoned, as are the limitations of one's actual past: 'But a space exists where everything that might have been / can still be summoned up and slotted in...'

The poems are not analyses, not observations, but the delivery of oxygen to things that would not otherwise have life at all. Of course there are concrete details, but they emerge out of the consciousness of the complicated persona, the figure that binds together the material of the poem. So, in 'An Own Way', the oilcloth, the laying of the table – for the dinner, but also for the wake of the speaker – are not concrete things or events, but rather thoughts in the mind of the poem's speaker. And when history is used, as in 'The Way It Goes' or 'Imperial Measure', it is the diminutive, rather than the grand narrative that is being written. The hypothesising is taken to fascinating lengths in 'Or to Come'. It takes some confidence (pardon me) to undertake a graveyard poem, especially one as experimental as this. Vona Groarke, for all the quietness, formality and care of her method, carries it off tremendously well.

There are some beautiful lines, as the following from 'Or to Come': 'The dear bouquets will have sweated a film of rust / inside their plastic domes, and the bare bones / of a handful of wild flowers in a jamjar hold their own.' The reader is lured, partly by the precedent of other famous graveyard poems, and partly by the precision of the imagery in this one, into thinking of the poet, or speaker, in a particular graveyard, meditating on the last things. Suddenly, one is brought up short, by Groarke's characteristic 'try this one for size' mode, and made to think of the poem as a set of devices and figures: 'It could be a churchless graveyard with a stile'; and later, 'Or an acre that knows the steady traffic of Sundays' / early masses'. There is also the intertextualism of the nod to the Ulyssean unknown man at the graveside that catapults this sombre and distinguished genre into modernity.

The indifference in this collection to whether a thing occurred in what we call fact, history, nature or reality on the one hand, or in the mind of the poet, the reader, or the page on the other, is significant. The hypothetical quality of many of the scenarios is connected to the collection's interest in writing and in doing some patient, diminutive work that is barely there to begin with, but that ends up in something durable. In several poems, most obviously in 'Oranges', the speaker, like Mrs. Ramsay in *To The Lighthouse*, looks in at her life, and sees it blazing and guttering in the moment it takes to see it. Vona Groarke has worked to create verbal patterns that are commensurate with the elusiveness and transience of such moments, real and imagined, and the result is formidable.

Dennis O'Driscoll opens his *Exemplary Damages* with the superb 'Out of Control', an address to mothers, telling them to keep on worrying about their children: 'Lie warily, mothers, where, / eighteen years before, conception / took place in the black of night, / a secret plot; / wait restlessly, / as if for a doctor's test, / to find out whether / you are still with child.' O' Driscoll is a real poet: his lines stay with you, and crop up unbidden in your mind as you go about your day. I find that the corpse 'sprouting thick fungal whiskers' of the poem 'Either' – from *Weather Permitting* – often make me feel queasy as I walk down the road.

Many readers find that O'Driscoll maintains a cool distance from his human subjects. This collection strikes me as above all humane. While the tone of the poems often comes across on first reading as satiric or mocking, what is actually very striking here is the affection for other humans, with all their faults and oddities. The absence of God is mourned in this collection ('Missing God'), not on theological grounds, but for the dignity and warmth that belief in him gave to ordinary humans and their daily lives: 'His grace is no longer called for / before meals: farmed fish multiply / without His intercession...' Here the poet almost replaces Him, and looks benignly and even lovingly on the most mundane of lives.

'Love Life' is a particularly good poem, which marvels at the sheer effort that goes into mating, the dedication of time and energy to the satisfaction of importunate instincts. In 'The Lads', some working men in a canteen dream of exoticism and Thailand, but the poems themselves stay closer to home, and find interest in the readily available. 'Full Flight' deals with people in airports and on airplanes, but all of O'Driscoll's emphasis, in the attention he pays to overhead bins and carry-on-bags, is on the way these passengers keep the sublime at bay. I suppose some readers will find the tone of these poems sardonic, unsentimental, even satiric. They strike me as affectionate and curious.

While O'Driscoll mostly deals with middle class life and modernity, there are some other figures in the landscape. The characters in poems like 'In Town', 'Remainders', 'Calling the Kettle' and 'Years After' are, indeed, 'remainders' of a bygone era, wandering, like the senile population of 'High Spirits', through modern life. Just as the sexual instincts of 'Love Life' keep on welling up in generation after generation, in those reared on Playstations as surely as those raised on embroidery, so old age and death are always modern, always with us, whether we like it or not: diseases on the dancefloor of 'Saturday Night Fever', and death in a 'digital epoch.'

In one of the best poems in this book, 'The Clericals', O'Driscoll produces a lovely, funny and observant elegy for the lost ways of pre-computer office life, for the carbon paper, the leaf tea, the adding-machine, and for the women who performed these jobs, whose unsung daily (and nightly) lives are brilliantly commemorated:

> Your youth was snatched from your nail-varnished grasp,
> lasting no longer than the push-button hall lights in red-brick
> houses where you returned by taxi in a pay-day's early hours...

Again, the quotidian detail is delightful, the attention to the old technologies that once upon a time dictated the ways in which life was lived and days were spent. O'Driscoll knows that life is in the details. He seems to be offering not just an anthropology of the adjacent and the everyday, but also the history of the only-just-past.

Adrian Frazier

Life in Leitrim

Vincent Woods, **Lives and Miracles** (drawings by Charles Cullen), Arlen House, 2002, €20.

Gallery now has a competitor in the West in the design of beautiful poetry books: Arlen House. Vincent Woods' collaboration in *Lives and Miracles* with his fellow member of Aosdána, the artist Charles Cullen, is a little treasure for bookshelves, the postmodern equivalent of a work of medieval hagiography and emblems, like the poems themselves.

Vincent Woods has been broadcaster, playwright (*At the Black Pig's Dyke, Song of the Yellow Bittern, On the Way Out*), poet (*The Colour of Language*), and editor. It is tempting, and contradictory, to say that as a playwright he reminds one that he is essentially a poet, the language being so choice; while his poems remind one that he is essentially a playwright.

Shakespeare famously is nowhere in his plays, but in his poems he's front and centre, the older man frankly loving a waster, or having his entrails twisted by the dark lady. Vincent Woods is not so candidly in evidence in this collection. He is certainly nothing like the unfortunate dunce of the lead-off sequence, *The Life and Miracles of Christy McGaddy*. This is a parodic Leitrim version of a saint's life. Stages on his life's journey have RC titles like 'The Assumption,' 'The Annunciation,' or 'His First Miracle':

> His first miracle was his best:
> He survived three years in the churn
> And seven at his mother's breast.

The poem is characteristic Woods in the way the rhyme brings it all home, and Leitrim is the glass in which the sorrow and comedy of immemorial human depravity is seen. It appears that it wasn't just in Missouri, where I grew up, but also in peasant Catholic Leitrim that well-grown boys would pull their mother behind a door to feed at the breast.

Cullen's drawing to illustrate 'His Father's Wake' – Christy McGaddy, somewhat like Christy Mahon in The Playboy, brains his father in a field – is wonderfully speedy, indicative, and sure-handed in laying out the scene. Woods' verses also imitate offhand haste:

> I thought he was restin',
> He said at the wake;
> When I went to rouse him
> I hit him with the rake...
>
> ...
>
> ...Isn't it funny he's dead.
> You'll have a cigarette.
> Hadn't he a lot of hair all the same
> For a dirty auld get.

But this is an art that hides art, a northern poetry like Kavanagh's that makes postmodernist play with traditional forms.

Equally commendable are the poems about the coal-mining era of Leitrim, as is the sequence which bookends *Lives and Miracles*, 'Scenes from the Black Valley (A Harlot's Progress)'! This is a most enjoyable collection from a superb writer who relishes the oblique and aesthetic point of view on life as she is known in Leitrim.

Notes on Contributors

Fergus Allen's most recent collection, *Mrs Power Looks Over the Bay*, was published by Faber & Faber in 1999.
Gary Allen's latest collection, *Languages*, was published in 2002 by Flambard/Black Mountain Press. He has had poems published in magazines and anthologies in Ireland and Britain, including *Honest Ulsterman*, *Metre*, *THE SHOp*, and *London Magazine*.
Doug Anderson has written three books of poetry, *Bamboo Bridge*, *The Moon Reflected Fire*, and *Blues for Unemployed Secret Police*. He has also written fiction, criticism, plays and film scripts. He is at present at work on a memoir about the Vietnam War.
Ivy Bannister's poems appeared most recently in *The Sunday Tribune*. She participated in the Poetry Ireland Introductions series and the Rattlebag Poetry Slam, both in 2002. She also writes stories and plays, and has won the Francis MacManus, Hennessy and Mobil (Ireland) Playwriting Awards.
Leland Bardwell's collections of poetry include *The Mad Cyclist* (New Writers' Press, 1970), and *The White Beach: New & Selected Poems 1960-1988* (Salmon, 1998). Her novels include *Girl on a Bicycle* (Co-Op Books, 1977), and *Mother to a Stranger* (Blackstaff Press, 2002). She is a member of Aosdána.
Gerard Beirne mentors in Creative Writing for the Manitoba Writers' Guild. His collection of poems *Digging My Own Grave* was published by Dedalus . His novel *The Eskimo in the Net* is published by Marion Boyars Publishing (2003).
Denise Blake is a poet and translator of Cathal Ó Searcaigh. She has been published widely, including in *THE SHOp* and *The Stinging Fly*.
Kevin Bowen is Director of the William Joiner Centre for the Study of War and Social Consequences at the University of Massachusetts. His most recent collection, *Eight True Maps of the West: New and Selected Poems* is published by Dedalus in 2003.
Mary Branley's first collection, *A Foot in the Tide* was published by Summer Palace Press in 2002. She has also written *Silk Kimono* (Sligo, The Factory Performance Place, 1995); and co-ordinated *Charlie Barley and all his friends*, an anthology of traveller children's nursery rhymes (Kids Own Publishing Partnership, 2001). She is a member of the Scríobh Literary Festival committee.
Deirdre Brennan's collections are *I Reilig na mBan Rialta* (1974); *Scoileanna Geala* (1989); and *The Hen Party* (Lapwing, 2001).
Lucy Brennan was born in Dublin, educated in Cork, and now lives in Whitby, Ontario. Her first collection was *Migrants All* (Watershed Books, 1999), and her work has been anthologised both in Canada and in Ireland.
Michael Brophy's work has been published in a range of magazines and anthologies, including Marian Forde's recent anthology for the Junior Certificate, *Rhyme & Reason*.
David Butler's translations of Fernando Pessoa are due from Dedalus in 2004.
Moya Cannon's collections are *Oar* (2000) and *The Parchment Boat* (1997), both from Gallery. She is a previous editor of *Poetry Ireland Review*.

Clíodhna Carney lectures in Old and Middle English in NUI, Galway.
Melanie Challenger graduated from Oxford in 2000. She is the youngest writer to date to receive an Arts Council *Investment in Artists* award.
Michael Coady lives in Carrick-on-Suir. He has published three collections with Gallery Press and is a member of Aosdána. A new collection is due in 2003.
Denis Collins is Artistic Director of Wexford Arts Centre and a partner in Wexford publishers, THE WORKS. In December 1999 he won the traditional section in the Francis Ledwidge Poetry Competition. He featured at the Poetry Ireland Introductions series in 2000, and was short-listed for the SeaCat / Poetry Ireland Award in 2001.
Patrick Cotter is Director of the Munster Literature Centre. His most recent publication is *The True Story of Aoife and Lir's Children* (Three Spires Press).
Tommy Curran's poetry has been most recently published in *THE SHOp* and *Bongos of the Lord* (Japan).
Bei Dao, born in Peking in 1949, was nominated for the Nobel Prize for literature in 1993. His books in translation include his collected poems *The August Sleepwalkers* (1989), *Old Snow* (1992), and *Forms of Distance*, all published by Anvil, and the collection of stories *Waves* (Heinemann, 1987).
John F Deane's collection *Manhandling the Deity* will be published by Carcanet in July, 2003.
Annie Deppe's first collection, *Sitting in the Sky*, was published this year by Summer Palace Press.
Nguyen Qui Duc is the author of *The Time Tree: Selected Poems* (Curbstone Press, 2003).
George Evans is the author of five books of poetry, most recently *The New World* (Curbstone, 2002). His poetry, fiction, essays and translations (from Spanish and Vietnamese) have been published in magazines throughout the US, as well as in Australia, England, France, Japan, and Vietnam.
Adrian Frazier is the director of the MA in Writing and the MA in Drama and Theatre Studies at NUI, Galway
Kieran Furey's work has appeared in *THE SHOp*, *West 47*, *The Burning Bush*, and *Poetry Scotland*, among other outlets. He is a past winner of the Dún Laoghaire International Poetry Competition (Spanish language category), and of the William Allingham Short Story Competition.
Giles Goodland is currently Senior Assistant Editor of the Oxford English Dictionary. His work has been widely published in magazines and anthologies, and in 2001 he received the K. Blundell Trust Award. His latest book, *A Spy in the House of Years*, was published by Leviathan Press, also in 2001.
Rody Gorman's collections include *Fax and Other Poems* (Polygon, 1996) and *Shlí Cualann* (Coiscéim, 2002).
Eamon Grennan teaches at Vassar College, and was the 2002 Heimbold Professor of Irish Studies at Villanova University. His most recent books are *Still Life with Waterfall* (Gallery, 2001); and *Facing the Music: Irish Poetry in the 20th Century* (Creighton University Press, 1999).
Danny Hardisty was born in West Yorkshire in 1978. His poems have

appeared in several publications in the UK.
Rita Ann Higgins's *Sunnyside Plucked: New & Selected Poems* (Bloodaxe, 1996) was a Poetry Books Society Recommendation. Her latest collection is *An Awful Racket* (Bloodaxe, 2001).
Lynda Horgan is a member of the fia rua writers group in Killarney. She graduated from the Limerick school of Art and Design in 1999.
Peter Jankowski, with Brian Lynch, is the translator of Paul Celan's *65 Poems* (Raven Arts Press).
Carolyn Jess has been published in *The Lonely Poets' Guide to Belfast* and *Carousel*, a Co. Down Poetry Anthology. A filmmaker, composer and photographer, she is currently attempting to publish her first poetry collection, *Inroads*.
Fred Johnston was born in Belfast in 1951. Founder of The Western Writers' Centre, his most recent collection of poems is the sequence *Paris Without Maps* (Northwords). He is also working on his second CD album, comprising his own and traditional songs. *Tracé de Dieu*, a novella, will be published in French and English in the Autumn.
Aileen Kelly grew up in England and is now an adult educator in Melbourne. Her poetry is widely published in Australia and elsewhere, and has won awards such as the Mary Gilmore Award and the Vincent Buckley Prize. Her latest book, *City and Stranger*, was recently published by Five Islands Press.
Jesse Lee Kercheval was born in France and raised in Florida. She is the author of five books, including the novel *The Museum of Happiness*. Her second poetry collection *Dog Angel* is forthcoming from the University of Pittsburg Press. Her poetry and fiction have appeared in the United States, Europe and Australia.
Ger Killeen is Professor of English Literature & Writing at Maryhurst University in Oregon. He is the author of two collections of poetry, *A Wren* (Bluestem Press, 1990), and *A Stone That Will Leap Over The Waves* (Trask House, 1999). He is a member of the Editorial Board of *Free Verse* .
Ann Killough's poems and reviews have been published in *Fence, Poems & Plays, Poet Lore, Plainsongs, THE SHOp*, and elsewhere. She was a finalist for the 2000 Grolier Prize and for the 2001 Milton Award for Excellence in Poetry. Her full-length manuscript, *White Girl Falls in Love*, for which she is seeking a publisher, was just named a finalist for the Alice James Books *New York/New England* Award.
Brian Lynch, with Peter Jankowski, is the translator of Paul Celan's *65 Poems* (Raven Arts Press).
Alice Lyons was born in Paterson, New Jersey and has lived in Ireland since 1998. She is the recipient of the Patrick Kavanagh Award for 2002, and an award from the Academy of American Poets.
Joan McBreen has published two poetry collections, *The Wind Beyond the Wall* (Story Line Press, 1990), and *A Walled Garden in Moylough* (Story Line Press and Salmon,1995). She is the editor of *The White Page / An Bhileog Bhán* (Salmon, 1999). *Winter in the Eye: New and Selected Poems* has just been published, also by Salmon.

Medbh McGuckian's collections of poetry include *The Flower Master* (1982, Oxford University Press, 1982; republished by Gallery, 1993); *Marconi's Cottage* (Gallery Press, 1991); *Selected Poems* (Gallery Press, 1997); and *Drawing Ballerinas* (Gallery Press, 2001). Her awards include The Cheltenham Award, The Alice Hunt Bartlett Prize, and the Bass Ireland Award for Literature. *Marconi's Cottage* was shortlisted for the Irish Times/Aer Lingus Irish Literature Prize for Poetry in 1992. She is a member of Aosdána.

Paul Maddern was born in Bermuda of Irish and Cornish stock. A graduate of Queen's University, Ontario, this is his first published work.

Giovanni Malito's publication credits include *Acumen*, *The Cork Review*, *Poetry Scotland*, *The Shop*, *Thumbscrew*, and *The Magazine*. He is editor of the literary broadsheet *The Brobdingnagian Times*.

Fred Marchant is a professor of English at Suffolk University in Boston, MA, and is the director of the creative writing program. His most recent collection, *House on Water, House in Air: New and Selected Poems*, was published by Dedalus in 2002.

David Meagher works as a psychiatrist in Limerick city.

Eugenio Montale (1896-1981) was born in Genoa. He is the author of nine collections of poetry, including the controversial *Posthumous Diary*. He also published numerous translations of verse, prose and drama, as well as hundreds of articles on literature, music and society. He was awarded the Nobel Prize for Literature in 1975.

Art Murphy has been published n a variety of journals, including *The Burning Bush*, *Cyphers*, *Metre*, *Honest Ulsterman*, and *The New Welsh Review*.

Gerard Murphy is a novelist and poet. Born in Cork, his first novel *Once in a New Moon* was published in 1997 by Dufour Editions, and his second novel is due out in 2004. He is currently compiling a collection of poetry.

Mary O'Donoghue lives and teaches in Boston. Her first collection, *Tulle*, was published by Salmon in 2001, and she is currently completing her second. She was selected as the Hennessy/Sunday Tribune New Irish Writer of the Year in 2001.

Ciaran O'Driscoll has published five collections of poetry, the latest of which is *Moving On, Still There: New and Selected Poems* (Dedalus, 2001). He has also recently published a childhood memoir, *A Runner Among Falling Leaves* (Liverpool University Press). In January 2000, he was awarded the Patrick and Katherine Kavanagh Fellowship in Poetry.

Nessa O'Mahony's poetry has appeared in a number of Irish, UK and American periodicals, including *Windows*, *Fortnight*, *Asylum*, and *Atlanta Review*, and has also been broadcast by RTE. Her first poetry collection, *Bar Talk*, was published by iTaLiCs Press in 1999.

William Oxley's publications include *Collected Longer Poems* (Salzburg University Press, 1994), and *Selected Poems* (Rockingham Press, 2001). A former member of the General Council of the Poetry Society and ex-assistant editor of *Acumen*, he is the also the founder of the Long Poem Group.

Jo Pestel participated in the Poetry Ireland Introductions series in 2002. She is published in journals in Ireland and the UK.

Aimée Sands is a poet and documentary filmmaker living in Boston. She is co-director of the Brookline Poetry Series, and an MFA candidate in poetry at Bennington College.

Knute Skinner's latest collection is *Stretches* (Salmon 2002).

Jo Slade has published three collections of poetry, including her most recent, *Certain Octobers* (Salmon and Edition Eireanna, 1997). She is the Limerick County Council Poet in Residence for 2002/2003, and is a member of the Limerick Fourfront Poets group.

John E Smelcer's poetry books include *Without Reservation* (Truman State University Press, 2003), *Riversongs* (CPR, 2001), and *Songs From an Outcast* (UCLA, 2000).

T Michael Sullivan is the coordinator of the William Joiner Center's Writers' Workshop at the University of Massachusetts, Boston. He has read his poetry in the Boston area and been published in local literary journals. He holds an M.A. from University College, Dublin.

Huu Thinh lives in Hanoi where he is a member of the National Assembly of Vietnam, Editor-In-Chief of the literary magazine *Van Nghe*, and General Director of the Writers' Association. He has published five books of poetry, winning numerous awards for his work.

Eliot Weinberger, along with Iona Man-Cheong, translated Bei Dao's collection *Unlock* (New Directions, 2000) into English.

Susan Wicks works part-time as a lecturer in Creative Writing for the University of Kent in Canterbury, where she directs the Creative Writing Programme. Her collection, *The Clever Daughter* (Faber & Faber, 1996), was a PBS Choice and shortlisted for both the T.S. Eliot and the Forward Prize. Her novels are *The Key* and *Little Thing*, both from Faber & Faber.

Anna Woodford received, in 2003, a Hawthornden Fellowship and an Arvon / Jerwood Apprenticeship. Her collection *The Higgins' Honeymoon* was published by Driftwood Publications in 2001.

Vincent Woods's stage plays include *At the Black Pig's Dyke* and *Song of the Yellow Bittern*; and for radio, *The Leitrim Hotel*. His poetry is collected as *The Colour of Language* (Dedalus, 1994). His awards include The Stewart Parker Award for Drama; the PJ O'Connor Award for Radio Drama; and the MJ McManus Award for Poetry. A member of Aosdána. His latest collection of poetry is *Lives and Miracles* (Arlen House, 2003).

Howard Wright is a lecturer in Art History at the University of Ulster, Belfast. His work has recently appeared in *Other Poetry*, *Northwords*, *Magma*, and *Leviathan*. A selection of 12 poems will be published in *New Soundings* (Blackstaff Press) at the Queen's Festival in October 2003.

Daisy Zamora, born in Nicaragua, was a combatant in the National Sandinista Liberation Front (FSLN) during the Nicaraguan revolution; was program director and voice of the clandestine Radio Sandino; and Vice-Minister of Culture. The author of many books of poetry, she is a well-known political activist and advocate for women's rights. Her latest collection in English is *The Violent Foam: New and Selected Poems* (Curbstone, 2002), translated by George Evans.

Books Received

Ed. by Pierre Dubrunquez, *poésie 2003*, No. 96 / Février.
Takaha Shugyo, *Selected Haiku* (ed. and translated by Hoshino Tsunehiko and Adrian Pinnington), Furansudo.
All Because of a Toothbrush, Heartland Press, Longford County Council/ Longford County Library and Arts Services.
Brian G D'Arcy, *Tha Shein Ukrosh/Indeed the Hunger*, Bellasis Press.
Ed. By Speer Morgan, *The Missouri Review*, Volume XXV, No. 2, 2002.
Ed. by Herbert Leibowitz, *Parnassus*, Volume 26, No.2.
Michael Begnal, *The Lakes of Coma*, Six Gallery Press.
Translated by Ernest Bryll, *Three Contemporary Irish Writers: Anthony Cronin, Anne Haverty and Dermot Healy*, UAM Motivex, Poznan, 2002.
James E.F. Pugh, *Just Another Buffalo*.
Roger McGough, *Everyday Eclipses*, Penguin.
Margaret Moore, *What The Wind Scatters*, Lapwing
Mary Melvin Geoghegan, *The Bright Unknown*, Lapwing.
Charles Hodbay, *Elegy for a Sergeant : A Poem for Voices*, Lapwing.
John Minihan & Gabriel Rosenstock, *Forgotten Whispers*, Anam Press.
Ciaran Carson, *Breaking News*, Gallery Books.
Rainer Maria Rilke, *The Life of the Virgin Mary* (translated by Christine McNeill), Dedalus (Waxwing Series No. 2).
Ed. by Robert Minhinnick, **Poetrywales**, Volume 38, No.4, Spring 2003.
Bernard O'Donoghue, *Outliving*, Chatto & Windus.
Vernon Watkins, *Poems for Dylan*, Gomer.
Chris Considine, *Learning To Look*, Peterloo Poets.
Ian Crockett, *Blizzards of the Inner Eye*, Peterloo Poets.
Ed. by Michael Begnal, *The Burning Bush*, Number Nine, Spring 2003.
Red Banner, Issues 14 and 15.
Tessa Ransford, *Scottish Selection*, Akros Publications.
Tessa Ransford, *Indian Selection*, Akros Publications.
Tessa Ransford, *Natural Selections*, Akros Publications.
Tessa Ransford, *Noteworthy Selection*, Akros Publications.
James Fenton, *An Introduction to English Poetry*, Penguin Books.
Ed. by Dr. Peter Thomas, *Scintilla* 7, 2003, Usk Valley Vaughan Association.
Gerald Dawe, *Lake Geneva*, Gallery Books.
Rosita Boland, *Dissecting The Heart*, Gallery Books.

Previous Editors of *Poetry Ireland Review*

John Jordan 1-8	Spring 1981 – Autumn 1983
Thomas McCarthy 9-12	Winter 1983 – Winter 1984
Conleth Ellis & Rita E. Kelly 13	Spring 1985
Terence Brown 14-17	Autumn 1985 – Autumn 1986
Ciaran Cosgrove 18-19	Spring 1987
Dennis O'Driscoll 20-21	Autumn 1987 – Spring 1988
John Ennis & Rory Brennan 22-23	Summer 1988
John Ennis 24-25	Winter 1988 – Spring 1989
Micheal O'Siadhail 26-29	Summer 1989 – Summer 1990
Máire Mhac an tSaoi 30-33	Autumn 1990 – Winter 1991
Peter Denman 34-37	Spring 1992 – Winter 1992
Pat Boran 38	Summer 1993
Seán Ó Cearnaigh 39	Autumn 1993
Pat Boran 40-42	Winter 1993 – Summer 1994
Chris Agee 43-44	Autumn/Winter 1994
Moya Cannon 45-48	Spring 1995 – Winter 1995
Liam Ó Muirthile 49	Spring 1996
Michael Longley 50	Summer 1996
Liam Ó Muirthile 51-52	Autumn 1996 – Spring 1997
Frank Ormsby 53-56	Summer 1997 – Spring 1998
Catherine Phil Mac Carthy 57-60	Summer 1998 – Spring 1999
Mark Roper 61-64	Summer 1999 – Spring 2000
Biddy Jenkinson 65-68	Summer 2000 – Spring 2001
Maurice Harmon 69-72	Summer 2001 – Spring 2002
Michael Smith 73-75	Summer 2002 – Winter 2002/3